£6.95 - £50

CAREERS IN

JOURNALISM

Simon Kent

eighth edition

**KOGAN
PAGE**

First published in 1981
Second edition 1986
Third edition 1988
Fourth edition 1989
Fifth edition 1992
Sixth edition 1994
Seventh edition 1996
Eighth edition 1997

Kogan Page Limited
120 Pentonville Road
London N1 9JN

© Kogan Page, 1981, 1986, 1988, 1989, 1992, 1994, 1996, 1997

British Library Cataloguing in Publication Data

A CIP record for this book is available from the British Library.

ISBN 0 7494 2389 7

Typeset by Kogan Page Ltd
Printed and bound in Great Britain by Clays Ltd, St Ives plc

Contents

Free newspapers; Press agencies; Jobs overseas; Press photography; Press and public relations officers (PRs); Government press services; Publicists, Advertising

1 Introduction

Is this the Job for You?

- [ ] Are you observant and interested in world affairs or local affairs?

- [ ] Can you work to a high level of accuracy?

- [ ] Can you write good English with correct grammar and punctuation?

- [ ] Are you good with people and do you have fantastic communication skills?

- [ ] Are you analytical and discerning, able to grasp and investigate a new subject quickly?

- [ ] Can you work irregular hours?

- [ ] Are you calm and imperturbable?

- [ ] Can you recognise a good story or find new angles on everyday subjects?

- [ ] Can you work well under pressure to fixed deadlines?

- [ ] Are you assertive and confident?

Journalism is one of the most exciting areas of work you can get involved in. It spans all other activities and society itself, following new developments, criticising and contributing to current issues throughout the world. Journalists need to know about the hottest news stories and be at the cutting edge of nationwide and worldwide opinion. Tomorrow's society will be information rich, dependent upon the talents of people who can explain events, ideas and products. Journalists will be in the vanguard of every step forward, publicising and analysing everything around them.

For some people, the image of the working journalist is a heavy-drinking, inconsiderate hack, more concerned about getting an exposé or a quote from those in the news than objectively explaining current events. The public do not always have a very high regard of the profession, holding journalists in very low esteen – higher only than politicians. However, this stereotype is becoming harder to find. Today's professional journalist is respectable and intelligent, frequently office based and as knowledgeable about his or her subject as anyone else involved in the area they are reporting on. Journalists are no longer purely paper based, but comfortable with all media.

The working life of the journalist has changed radically over the last ten years and continues to do so on a monthly and sometimes weekly basis. Changes in printing technology revolutionised production in the 1980s, but this simply prefigured more radical changes in the industry this decade. The shock to the system is still being worked through. Technology is increasing at break-neck speed and while no one can predict what will be achieved in the next few years, journalism will be a volatile and exciting area of employment well into the future.

Fleet Street may still retain some glamour and is still quoted in reference to the industry, but the last paper produced there was in 1989. Aside from the national newspapers, journalists work on large provincial, daily and weekly newspapers, trade and technical newspapers and magazines, political, educational and sporting papers, magazines devoted to particular interests and hobbies, entertainment magazines, women's magazines and even children's comics. All of these subjects can also be found in other media from TV to the Internet. Indeed, newspapers are no longer competing only with each other for readers but are trying to attract audiences from the expanding TV network – in cable, satellite, terrestrial and digital formats – radio and the Internet.

From modest beginnings in journalism came such great names as Edgar Wallace and Charles Dickens. Indeed, Dickens was so pleased to get his first pieces published that he wondered if he would get paid for them as well as having the thrill of seeing them in print! The range of opportunities for journalists has never been greater. Nor has it been more uncertain. You may enter the industry today with your sights fixed firmly on achieving editorship of a major publication in 20 years' time, only to find that the work of editors has completely changed by that time and the printed media themselves no longer operate in the way you are used to. Alternatively, you may find an opportunity to set up your own publication – the technology already exists for you to publish your own glossy magazine or newspaper relatively inexpensively. In short, if you have the right skills and maintain a journalist's sharp eye for a good story, there is no limit to where your career can go.

This book is published at a difficult time for many journalists. New technology has replaced many jobs; the BBC is restructuring their organisation; a new terrestrial TV channel has been launched and speculation is rife about the future of digital TV and radio. News reporting is constantly criticised for trivialising some issues and sensationalising or ignoring others. The use of technology in publishing is still not fully established and many workers are finding they are called upon to provide more text in less time with fewer resources available. The skills highlighted in this book remain constant but how you achieve those skills, how they relate to the job and the need for technological skills will be different for every individual.

This book begins by looking at some of the principal occupation areas for journalists. It gives useful tips for success in the industry in general and for specific organisations. It also looks at the future of the industry. There is a guide to the main journalism qualifications available, from whatever circumstances you are starting. At the end of the book there are useful address and suggestions for further reading.

Reportage:
a general overview of
the journalist's job

Whatever area of journalism you wish to work in, it is best to forget all ideas of a nine-to-five job. Fires, accidents, crimes and other newsworthy events happen at any time of the day or night and someone has to be there to cover the story. Staff journalists may work a shift system, which changes weekly, and sometimes includes early mornings and late nights. Freelances, photographers, regional and special correspondents are only a bleep or a mobile phone call away from having to produce exclusive copy on a story ready for the first issue next day.

There may be some regular reporting centred upon events which take place at specific times of the day. Law reporters cover court sessions which take place at fixed times – as do some sports writers. However, in both of these cases, such correspondents are more likely to be freelance, submitting copy as and when needed while also keeping abreast of current events.

What skills do you need?

Journalists should be observant first and foremost. They should have a natural interest in world affairs or the day-to-day events in the community they are writing about. Alternatively, in-depth and up-to-date knowledge of a particular subject may form the basis of a lucrative writing career. The emphasis is always on accuracy both in subject matter and in the use of English. A slapdash worker will not last long. One editorial office has two notices which set out the golden rules: 'GET IT RIGHT' and 'CHECK YOUR FACTS'. Inaccurate reporting will soon lose readers and the reporter will lose his or her job.

However, in certain parts of the media, these requirements may be less important than writing to the publication's style and for the readership or audience. The so-called 'tabloid' newspaper market cannot be commended for either its promotion of good English or clear, objective reporting. Sensationalism and hype appear to be the key to some newspapers' success and there is still an amount of lucrative work available in this area. The important point to bear in mind, whoever you write for, is to write the story at a suitable level for the readers. Readers will not look at your article if it is presented in a way which is unatractive to them and will not read all the way through if it fails to hold their attention. There is no point in providing an indepth analysis of a football match if readers just want to know who won.

Reporters must be aware of public opinion. Journalists need to know what the public are thinking and sometimes predict what they will think about a certain event. It is difficult to know whether journalists dictate public reaction or whether they are simply pandering to what the public wants to believe. Either way, a reporter must have 'a nose for news' – the ability to scent a big story where only a small one appears to exist and to discard stories which are of no importance.

Every journalist needs to be able to interview effectively, whether for an opinion piece for broadcast or simply to check facts. It is by no means an easy process. Most people meander rather than speak in sound bites, leaving the reporter to sift through a great deal of information to bring out the nub of a story. Journalists need to be analytical and logical, capable of assimilating complex subjects in a matter of minutes in order to get to grips with the important issues.

Tact is also a great requirement when dealing with interview situations. Prematurely cutting off interviewees might antagonise them. Asking the wrong question at the wrong time can jeopardise the entire interview. After all, these people are under no obligation to speak to you and asking personal questions may not go down too well. Equally, your subject may be shy or reticent when interviewed, and so need to be put at ease before talking on the subject.

Radio and TV interviewers are also up against the time factor. Not only must the interviewee say something germane to the subject, he or she must say it without running into the next item. In addition, listeners and viewers may get bored if an interview goes on for too long or does not cover new ground.

In all areas of journalism, calm is essential. Journalists are used to working under pressure – of deadlines, of getting the right story, of making contact with specific individuals – and you must be able to rise above this in order to write coherent copy at the end of the day. You'll need a certain doggedness and determination to get and follow up a story – though you will not need to be quite so ruthless as the reporters who are (sometimes unfavourably) portrayed in films and on TV.

Trade union membership

Trade unions used to operate a closed shop among journalists and newspaper production staff. However, while some employers still expect employees to join an appropriate union, it is rare to find employment being denied on these grounds. Many magazines and newspapers have de-recognised the unions, denying them the right to represent the workforce or to influence the pay and conditions of their members.

That said, there is still a strong case for union membership, since this will help to keep you in touch with issues which affect the workplace. Both the National Union of Journalists (NUJ) and the Chartered Institute of Journalists have accepted the new technology as part of the new way of working in journalism. Indeed, one of the NUJ's biggest campaigns in recent years has been to promote awareness and avoidance of repetitive strain injury and how to work safely with VDUs.

Members come from all areas of journalism – newspapers, broadcasting, book publishing, photography and public relations – and unions are particularly useful for freelance workers who may otherwise be isolated. One invaluable service provided by the NUJ is a 'Rate for the Job' feature wherein freelances state how much they are paid for specific articles, thus setting a standard for fellow members to refer to when negotiating their own terms with the same publication. Journalism students on recognised courses such as those validated by the National Council for the Training of Journalists (NCTJ), the Periodical Publishers Association (PPA) and the National Council for the Training of Broadcast Journalists (NCTBJ) are eligible to join the NUJ. Trainees become members as soon as they start employment; pre-entry students and those starting off as freelance journalists can apply for temporary membership.

Membership not only confers recognition as a professional worker, but unions can also offer help and advice when dealing with all employers. They can help resolve disputes with employers and support any legal arguments or actions which become necessary. Membership may also offer access to privileged rates for pensions, savings, insurance and even equipment and while it may not find you employment directly, it will put you in a better position to know where vacancies are likely to occur.

Journalists and the law

The NUJ's membership card – or other forms of press identification – can secure benefits as part of the job. You may gain free access to theatres, films, trade exhibitions and events about which you are writing. But, contrary to popular belief, the press card is not a passport to unlimited freebies and irresponsible behaviour. The law applies to journalists as much as it does to anybody else. If a reporter, in order to obtain an interview with a person who is reluctant to be interviewed, climbs through an open window of that person's home, the reporter could be charged with trespass. Internationally, war correspondents are supposed to have 'protected' status (as non-combatants) but that does not stop them from getting killed or imprisoned if the country in which they are working doesn't like what they are reporting.

A reporter can be accused of contempt of court merely by publishing the content of documents which have been shown in open court. The courts are very suspicious of anything that looks like 'trial by newspaper', indeed there have been cases dismissed in the courts because press coverage has been thought too heavy handed to permit a fair trial. There are rules, too, about reporting cases involving juveniles, whose names may not be revealed unless the court agrees; the court may also direct no reporting of people's names in blackmail cases. Names of jurors may not be published; a judge may direct that certain evidence be withheld from publication.

Perhaps the greatest publicity a paper gets, and a kind it could well do without, is when it has been found guilty of publishing a libel. The question of what is or is not a libel is argued in court, and a successful litigant may receive substantial damages from a newspaper. In some instances, the Official Secrets Acts come into play. Sometimes information is 'leaked' to the press. If confidential matters, for example concerning the defence of the country, are involved, the reporter obtaining this information and the paper publishing it might well be charged under these Acts. It is hardly surprising that courses on the law are now intrinsic to journalism training.

The journalist's code of ethics

In other areas, the law is a little more hazy or may clash with the unwritten code of ethics for journalists. If an informant is interviewed by a reporter, should he or she (after having got the story) reveal the informant's whereabouts if the source doesn't want to be found? If they don't, they might be in trouble with authority; if they do, they are unlikely to get any more information from that source.

Another area of journalistic ethics covers information which is given to the press with an 'embargo date'. This often happens with press notices containing advance information intended for press publication. The information gives reporters and editors a chance to develop a story so that it can 'break' on a specified date. This class of information is not legally protected, but the embargo is observed by reporters and papers.

Similarly, the police may give information to a newspaper with the request that it is not published until they agree, or a local council may have indicated a confidential decision which they do not want publicised until they have 'cleared their own procedures'. It is not usual to report the names of victims of a road accident or an air crash until the relatives have been informed. Requests from informants should be adhered to whenever possible in order to prevent the paper from attracting criticism or confrontation and to ensure sources will continue to speak to the publication.

Complaints

When complaints are made about press treatment, the final arbiter for newspapers is the Press Complaints Commission. This organisation deals with all complaints about alleged breaches of journalistic or editorial ethics, such as doubtful methods of obtaining news copy, major mistakes in reporting, deliberately biased reporting, invasion of privacy, harassment and so on. After the matter has been investigated, it is adjudicated and the results made public. Complaints about items broadcast on BBC and independent networks are investigated by the Broadcasting Complaints Commission while matters relating to standards of broadcasting are handled by the Broadcasting Standards Council and the Independent Television Commission (ITC).

Naturally, as a professional, well trained and honest journalist, the only time you will come across these organisations will be when you are reporting on complaints, rather than contesting them.

Paper work: traditional newspaper work

The traditional career path in newspapers was to start as a reporter with a small local or provincial paper and to work your way up, taking on more important stories, moving into bigger publications and assuming more editorial responsibility. In other words, you'd start by being told what to write about and work your way into a position where you were telling other people what to write about and how to write it.

Working on a local newspaper

Local newspapers provide an excellent grounding for a career in journalism. Many publishing organisations employ newcomers on a training contract or offer a period of indentured employment which leads to a National Certificate or NVQ/ SVQ at Level 4. Some companies have their own in-house training schemes which are also open to external employees.

Working for a small press offers extensive experience and an insight into many areas of producing a daily or weekly newspaper. Here you will see all life, high and low, which can be an education in itself. You will be able to see how news stories are gathered, features are commissioned and understand the relationship between copy and advertising – the chief source of income for most publications. Some journalists remain with local or district papers for the whole of their careers and are content to do so, becoming features editor or chief editor. (The structure of a typical newspaper is shown on page 11.) The size of area a local newspaper covers will vary according to the population of the district: it will have a readership radius of a mile or two if it is published in a heavily built-up area (eg in one of the

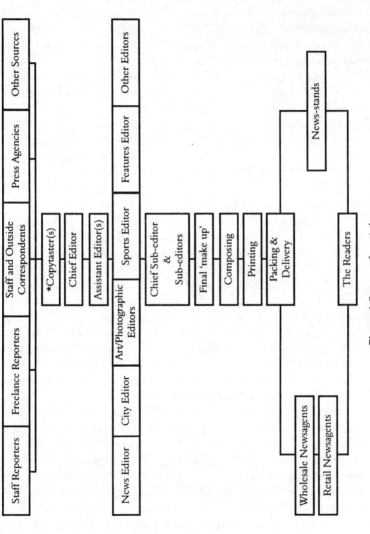

Figure 1 *Structure of a typical newspaper*

*Looks at the news when it first comes in and assesses its value

London boroughs) or spread its coverage over half a county if it serves a predominantly rural area.

Junior reporters have an opportunity to learn many journalistic and editorial jobs around the office such as subbing (sub-editing), layout and caption writing. They may also have to sub their own copy if asked, in order to bring out a point in more detail, cut the length of the report or article, or play down some aspects in favour of others. There may also be some proofreading and rewriting to do on outside contributions or special feature writing.

As a junior reporter, you may be sent out to cover diverse assignments. A glance at any local newspaper will show the kind of stories that are covered. Significant court cases and local council business are reported in almost every issue. One week the paper may carry only a list of planning applications, the next week a full report on one particularly controversial application where the environment is threatened. A really 'hot' subject, such as knocking down houses to build a bypass or the establishment of an industry in an otherwise residential area, may continually appear in the paper over several weeks.

A reporter may be in attendance at a civic reception, a meeting of the Chamber of Commerce, a road safety demonstration or a residents' association meeting – these are all regular diary items, perhaps not dramatic, but essential 'food' for the paper. There may be events which have more than local interest – a railway accident, a local visit by royalty or a well-known political figure, even a murder. On occasions, the national media will approach the local press for information and contacts, and even for a reporter who can provide copy.

Accidents, fires, hospitalisations, sudden deaths, public disturbances, protests and meetings are reported every week and can sometimes provide dramatic copy, but less startling events also get coverage. Weddings, funerals, retirements – anything which may be of interest to residents will find a place in the local paper. There may be performances of the amateur dramatic or operatic groups to report, what's on at the cinema, perhaps a book to review – particularly if the author is a local resident. This may appear mundane, but news reporting is not always dramatic, ground-breaking or scandalous – even on national papers. Again, the great thing about working on a local paper is that it introduces you to the nuts and bolts of putting together a paper while offering glimpses into the more high profile side of the industry.

Case Study

Alison *is a features editor on a national daily newspaper. She started out in the industry just under 20 years ago.*

'I started out on a local newspaper. One of my responsibilities was to compile the weekly events listings. It was mind-numbingly boring but I was still getting the satisfaction of seeing my work in print each week. There was a lot of sub-editing work to do – summing up big events into a couple of sentences which would fit the style and size of the listing section.

Since I received all the information about events, I would be first in line if there were invitations to opening nights or presentations. I was able to review a few plays, was invited to the occasional press launch of a new product and sometimes had the chance to interview celebrities who were visiting the area. My editor was very demanding and could be very hard on journalists if their work wasn't up to scratch or if they made written mistakes. At the same time, he was very encouraging and frequently asked me to propose feature ideas which would tie in with local events. Gradually, I was given more reporting work to do until I was spending more time gathering information and interviewing people than I was in the office writing the stories.

There was one particular event in the area which attracted national coverage and while I was there for the local paper I met many people from the national dailies. Someone there mentioned there was the chance of a reporter's job with their paper so when I got back to the office I simply phoned up the paper and asked about the vacancy. Sure enough, they were interested in employing a new reporter. By now I had built up a good portfolio of work and was able to take the job.

I worked for the Home News section for about seven years before the position of section editor came up. In some ways I miss the daily challenge of finding a new story and chasing it, but at the same time I am able to control what will appear each day and to edit the reports which come in, which is equally satisfying.

Working on the nationals means constantly finding fresh angles on news stories. Regional papers take different stories almost every day, but there is a slower turnover of subjects on a national level. One story may run for weeks and your reader will quickly lose interest if you cannot bring anything new or inspiring to the subject.'

Working on a national newspaper

Having served some time at a local level, you may then be able to move to one of the larger circulation provincial papers in one of the big cities, such as Glasgow, Birmingham, Manchester or Liverpool. You can then move onwards and upwards to the nationals. As you progress, you will find you are asked to contribute across an increasingly narrow range of subjects. A local reporter may work on a political piece in the morning and an entertainment piece in the afternoon. A reporter for a large paper will be expected to contribute to one area only – current affairs, business news, arts and so on.

As the circulation figures increase, so too does the number of sources from which you will take information. Copy for the local press may be generated by talking to a few sources each week, whereas contributing to the national press means keeping up to date with what is happening nationwide and worldwide.

Larger sections of a newspaper, for example current affairs, home news and foreign news, have regular press conferences throughout the day in which editors discuss the news as it is breaking and decide how stories will be best covered in the following day's paper. Reporters will then be delegated to work on each story, following new developments, analysing events and researching background. A story which appears to have national importance in the morning may later prove to be a let-down. Many times, an off-the-cuff remark by an MP has provided substantial material for the next day's paper.

There may also be special editions or features which tie in with special events or specific advertisements in the paper. In this case, editors and journalists need to work to absolute deadlines and may have to exercise an enormous amount of tact when writing about the subject. On the one hand, a journalist's report must not be biased by the advertisement, while on the other, advertisers who are covered in an article will not appreciate negative criticism and may decide not to advertise with the publication in the future.

Sometimes a paper will change its front page overnight in order to keep up with the news as it breaks, and of course, in order to do this, there have to be journalists, sub-editors and layout staff working into the small hours of the morning.

Gaining a position on a national newspaper is not necessarily a gradual progression. National papers have always taken on specialist writers – and some reporters – with little track record in journalism. People from the business or the entertainment world bring their knowledge to the paper, giving the publication extra kudos and offering readers the opinion of people 'in the know'. You may have a special interest which already puts you in a similar position. Your interest needs to be detailed but general: someone with a sound general knowledge of music is more likely to find employment than someone who knows everything there is to know about American folk music but nothing about English pop music.

This trend has led to the growth in 'celebrity' columnists. A few years ago most papers carried perhaps one opinion piece from a famous person; today there are daily exclusives in which celebrities hold forth on everything from politics to television. This is a product of the readership wars and has unfortunately led to some cases where status and notoriety have replaced good writing skills.

Many journalists aspire to writing their own column – a piece where they can write about what is on their mind and put forward their own ideas on a particular subject. In many cases, being offered such a column means knowing the right people rather than proving your journalistic capability. Column writing can be extremely difficult. The freedom to speak on any subject at all leaves the writer wondering what to write about. All columnists have their own draw factor for their readers, otherwise why would readers want to know about the subject or be interested in what they have to say?

The proliferation of freelance journalists used by national papers plus the use of new technology mean that while the structure of a typical newspaper still follows the diagram on page 11, it is unlikely that you will find an individual worker in each position. Section editors on national papers can now receive features from freelances by e-mail, immediately paste them on to the page and construct their layout accordingly. This side-steps other editorial levels and has reduced the need for composition and layout staff.

It should also be noted that in recent years the readership wars have made the position of all staff more insecure. The number of changes in editorial staff among the broadsheets has been remarkable, as have the changes in design of many of the papers. Selling newspapers now does not rely purely upon clear, incisive and ground-breaking reports, but on the visual appearance of the paper and the value of the reader offer. The former development is hardly surprising. We live in a technological age where we can create striking imagery very easily. Faced with competition from exciting visual media, the Internet and even magazines, newspapers need to make sure their product grabs the reader as they pass the newsagents.

Case Study

Elizabeth *works for a firm of newspaper and magazine publishers.*

'When I first came here I was a bit worried because it was such a large concern and I felt a little overwhelmed at the vastness of it all. I soon found myself very much at home, though. It is a family business and they treat their employees very well. When I looked round my particular department I was impressed by the number of people who had stayed with the firm for so many years and would probably remain with it until they retired. I was glad, too, that there were young people in the department, some of them beginners like myself.

At first, I thought I was going to do nothing but secretarial work. I could type and do shorthand, and the department corresponded with the authors and freelance writers who contributed to the papers and magazines. One of the jobs I liked was writing to new authors, telling them that their work had been accepted – I felt I was sharing in their pleasure at placing their work! Through corresponding with writers, I learnt about royalties, copyright, film rights and other secondary rights and so on. There was some in-house training too.

Later, I was able to do a small amount of writing for some of the regular features which appeared in our women's magazines. We had outside contributors, but a number of staff writers as well. I did small pieces on cookery, costume jewellery, travel, and social pieces about people who were in the news.

Although we have a strong fiction list, and I once tried my hand at a few stories, it is our regular columns on topics such as royal occasions, the cinema, home decoration and cookery which interest me most. I was concerned with the fiction side in one way though – I kept the schedules, which meant I had to watch for the copy coming in on time, and follow copy through proof and printing to payment to the author.

On the feature articles and other contributions there is sub-editing to do and I undertake some of this work. It's sometimes necessary to cut the material to a more acceptable length or to change certain aspects of it, but this usually causes no trouble with the writers – as long as one explains to them first.

Most of my work is done inside the office, but I also report on fashion showings, film previews or trade fairs.

We are a happy team, and that's why I wouldn't want to move elsewhere.'

Glossy and special: the world of magazines and periodicals

National and local newspapers are geared up to put out a new product every day. On the face of it, this appears to be harder work than producing a publication which comes out once a month, but the pressures on magazines and periodicals to ensure their material is up to date and published on time also produces hard deadlines.

The production procedures for 'the glossies' which appear on newsagents' shelves each month mean that copy, photography and advertising need to be ready to go to the printers several days, and sometimes weeks, in advance of the publishing date. Therefore, it is extremely difficult to guarantee the information contained in the pages will be relevant and up to date. In addition, subjects covered in spring are already decided upon by the beginning of winter. If a magazine is sold on its up-to-the-minute insider information on a particular subject, or on its fashion content, problems immediately become apparent.

Thanks to technology, a magazine can be produced with very few staff. Even large organisations such as EMAP and IPC may employ teams of only half a dozen, or less, to pull together a magazine with hundreds of pages. Magazines and periodicals rely heavily on freelance contributions and full-time work here may be more about managing and co-ordinating a team of contributors than generating text. This reliance means that full-time staff, such as the magazine's commissioning editor, must have a firm grasp of the subject covered by the magazine and be able to develop the magazine's identity and maintain its readership. In any one publication there may be a number of 'contributing editors' responsible for both writing and editing the contents of certain sections. Such editors may be employed full time or as freelance workers. This structure means the maximum care and attention can be paid to each part of the magazine, rather than relying on one person to oversee the entire operation. Pay on the larger-circulation magazines, whether in house or freelance, can be very high, but then so are the standards required.

There are over 8,000 periodicals of all kinds in this country alone. They are published by over 150 periodical publishing companies, mainly in London and the Home Counties. They can be split into two kinds: lifestyle and trade magazines.

Lifestyle magazines

These publications are the ones you will see in any newsagent's. They may be targeted at a particular kind of person according to gender and age. There are comics and 'pop' magazines for children, a separate market for teenage girls, publications for women – from *Vogue* to the more down-to-earth *Women's Weekly* – GQ and *Arena* for men, and publications like *The Face* which are directed at young, fashion-conscious adults. The past few years have seen a marked development in the area of men's magazines – the publication of *Loaded*, for example, has spawned a whole new genre of 'Lads' magazines. There is also a new market in men's health magazines.

There are more magazines today which address lifestyle interests – music-orientated, club and DJ magazines, computer games and technology through to trains, boats and sporting activities. There has been a recent trend in magazines on 'The Unexplained', tying in with TV programmes such as The X Files. It is a mark of how easy technology has made magazine publishing that there are so many specialist magazines around – think of any activity, hobby or interest and you will find a magazine on the subject. It should be pointed out, however, that since some of these magazines sell off the back of one particular fashion or trend, once that trend is over, the magazine is likely to go too.

Trade magazines

Trade magazines usually do not appear in the newsagent's. They provide people within a specific industry with information and data for their everyday work. There are publications which cover grocery, hardware, china and glass, fancy goods, stationery, toys and games, goldsmiths, silversmiths and jewellery trades, catering and hotel-keeping, travel trades, wood and metal, furniture, iron, coal and steel, bakery and confectionery, shipping, the clothing and footwear trade, building and construction, office equipment, perfumery. These magazines are also interesting for readers with a general interest in the area who need current market prices, trends and expectations for the future. Other magazines include the following:

In-house magazines

These publications are produced within an organisation and distributed among staff. This is an effective communication tool to keep employees aware of what is going on companywide and to ensure information reaches all staff. Such publications can also provide effective external publicity.

Magazines produced by or for organisations and associations

Subscribers to health clubs, holiday clubs, professional associations or cultural activities may receive dedicated magazines to keep them informed of membership privileges or simply for general interest. Cultural, sports, recreational, scientific, technical, educational, social and even entertainment associations may supply publications to members as part of their membership privileges. Some of these are only news-sheets but others can be glossy magazines of some substance and prestige. These larger ones commission work and often employ full-time writers and editors.

Professional publications

These are produced for specific professional workers. There are publications for doctors, hospital staff, dentists, opticians, architects, engineers, lawyers, and economists. They are generally produced by people who already have a sound background in the relevant area. They will carry news and views as well as contemporary research in that specific area.

Some of these periodicals may be extremely academic and limited in their field of reference and indeed their readership. Publications which are based in academic institutions may provide a focal point for new research and thinking in that field, but may not actually offer any payment for articles submitted and published.

Getting started

Entry into this field of journalism is somewhat different from entry into the daily or provincial newspapers simply because of the specialist knowledge required. It is unlikely that you will find yourself writing for such a publication without already having a strong academic background in the subject area. However, you may find opportunities in administration and layout work within companies publishing these magazines.

Most publishers will look for a certain educational standard, usually one or two A-levels or equivalent, but it is estimated that 85 per cent of entrants to this area of the industry are graduates or postgraduates. That said, it is still possible to find work with only the ability to write good English and to be able to present it in the form of an article, feature or column to the satisfaction of the employer.

One method of entry is to submit freelance contributions to a magazine which interests you and, if you are successful in getting work accepted, make it known that you are looking for a staff job in this field. It is worth remembering that many posts are never advertised but go to people known to the editor. Some writers get jobs by being on the staff in a totally different capacity and on the spot when vacancies come up.

It does no harm to write a few letters on spec to editors of magazines you are interested in. If you do, send some examples of your writing to give them an idea of your ability – even if they have never been published. *Benn's UK Media Directory*, *Willing's Press Guide*, *The Writers' and Artists' Yearbook* and *The Writer's Handbook* are all annual publications that have up-to-date contact points for British and foreign periodicals.

Case Study

Peter *began in journalism as an editorial assistant with a group of trade periodicals. There were eight magazines in the group, but he worked for only one, the magazine dealing with baking and confectionery. The editor himself was not a baker or confectioner, but a good journalist and researcher who communicated his enthusiasm for the magazine to his subordinates. He was a great believer in in-house training.*

'At first I had to learn the ropes. My first job was to write short captions for photographs which were going into the magazine the following month. I always got them in plenty of time, but I soon found I was running out of ideas. The captions had to be bright, very short, and informative. I found I was constantly using the same phrases, so I sat beside a senior reporter who did a set of photographs for me and I soon learned the tricks.

The paper reported on most of the baking and confectionery exhibitions in the country. I went to some of these, at first with a senior reporter, just following him round, being introduced to the stand-holders as one of the magazine's new reporters. Naturally, I read his review of the exhibition and then was sent out on my own to report. The fact I'd been out with a senior and noted what he considered newsworthy, and how he subsequently prepared his material, gave me much more confidence than I might otherwise have had.

Next, we had a number of freelance contributors to the paper. They were not journalists but people in the trade. The articles they submitted were often too long and it was my job to edit them down. Again, a senior reporter showed me how the job should be done without irritating the contributor of the article, misrepresenting him, or leaving out important bits – or at least, bits which the contributor thought important.

After about two years I left the firm to take up a better appointment as journalist/feature writer, plus some editorial duties, with a travel promotion organisation. Here I found that my experience with picture caption writing was much appreciated; they also produced some of their own films and I did caption writing for these too.

I was sent on a number of outside visits – including food and drink, hotels, train, bus and air services, places to visit, theatres, opera and ballet. The sub-editing work was for brochures, press handouts and travel guides, and there were three house magazines. We also worked on guides to forthcoming events, from trade conferences and fairs to sporting fixtures. We all took a hand at proof-correcting, from galleys to page proofs. Fortunately, I had done quite a bit of this in my previous job, and again chased up copy and wrote the occasional 'filler'.

There was a good deal of research work as I think we were expected to be experts in every subject which might interest holidaymakers either from home or abroad, but having to do this gave me another useful experience – how to build up sources of information.'

Starting your own magazine

Of course, there is nothing to stop you from starting your own publication if you can find a new market and believe you can produce the right publication to fill the space. One Apple Mackintosh computer with QuarkXPress, Photoshop and a few other pieces of hard- and software will enable you to write and lay out each page with pictures to a very high quality. It is then simply a matter of sending an electronically produced film, plus colour photographs, to a printer to produce a high-quality magazine.

Many people who start magazines have already had experience in this area, from editing and designing the school or college magazine through to working for another magazine and seeing how the process works. As with all publications, if the idea is strong enough, it will attract readers and, as long as they are the right kind of readers, advertisers will pay for advertising space and make the publication a success.

A note on correspondents

Magazines rely on journalists with specialist knowledge whereas newspapers mainly employ people to cover a wider range of subjects, reflecting the more general interests of their readers. Occasionally, however, newspapers will seek to employ or train people who are or will become special correspondents.

Special correspondents cover subjects such as: politics, international relations, conflict and war, royalty, fashion, food, business, gardening, architecture, housing, the environment, technology, science, health, education, religious affairs, employment and careers, energy, local government and transport.

Journalists may find themselves becoming specialist correspondents through design or, more frequently, by accident. It may be a subject they already have knowledge about or an area which they simply find they are always covering. A local journalist given coverage of the courts will gradually build up a knowledge of how the system works and be able to offer an informed opinion on the subject. He or she may be able to offer these skills to a wider audience via the national press or be able to go freelance, reporting on significant stories as they occur.

Another example may be journalists who find they are always given artistic reviews – simply attending the theatre or art gallery on a regular basis will build up their vocabulary and experience of the area. Some journalists set out specifically to work in one area and will emphasise their special interest to an editor even if they end up writing a variety of articles.

Success in this field is particularly attractive since you are likely to be writing on a subject you love, thus combining work and pleasure. Take, for example, the job of the restaurant critic or the film critic:

they get to indulge in their passion (usually for free) and then write about the subject – in an unbiased way – afterwards. In addition, as you become more specialised in your writing, the people you are writing about will come to you in order to be written about. PR agencies will beat a path to your door to have their clients featured in one of your articles, or theatre and concert promoters will insist you pass judgement on their latest offering rather than some other journalist who doesn't have your experience.

Specialist jobs, such as that of a foreign correspondent, do not always appear quite so attractive – particularly if you are sent to cover armed combat in a dangerous part of the world. At the same time, being out there on the front line, working to ensure the rest of the world knows what is going on, is an invigorating and exciting assignment.

Travel writing has become very fashionable recently with seasoned world travellers using their skills and experiences to inform readers how to get the most from a visit, where to go and what to see. Travel writers frequently take their own photographs as well and are able to offer editors entire features – words and pictures at once. This area is extremely competitive because many people who go travelling assume they can write about it in a way which no one else can. While this is probably true, as with all special correspondents, they must be able to write about their subject in a way which people want to read.

Case Study

Shona *left university with a 2:1 in English and took a secretarial post in the offices of a national women's glossy magazine in London.*

'Some people thought I was mad to take the job. To begin with, they thought the job was "below" me because I had a good degree. A lot of people also thought it was a mistake as I had to move to London and it was extremely expensive living there. They said I should have taken a training course and got a proper qualification. But I wanted to work for this particular magazine and felt this was the ideal opportunity.'

While her job title was 'secretary', very soon Shona was doing much more than answering the phones and arranging meetings. As the publication reached the monthly 'press day' – when the entire copy of the magazine is sent to the printers – deadlines became shorter and the contributors and editors needed help in many different areas of the magazine. One day, Shona would help to collate a list of advertisers in the issue, the next she would be sent to collect some photos for a style feature.

'Dauluully, I saw all areas of the operation first hand,' Shona comments. 'I'd listen to the editors discuss and commission work from freelance writers, I'd be there when they decided which photos to use with a feature, and I'd be there when the sub-editors had to check up facts for some of the articles.'

On one occasion, Shona was sent on a location shoot for one of the fashion features. 'It was a fantastic experience,' she says. 'I was just there to help out – to carry some of the equipment and make sure the designer and photographer had everything they needed. The trip really taught me a lot about how to manage fashion shoots as well as what makes a good fashion feature.'

After 18 months with the magazine, Shona was given the opportunity to co-edit a fashion feature with one of the magazine's editors. The editor was so impressed with Shona's ideas and thorough research that she gave Shona the chance to do her own feature for the next issue. 'That was really nerve-racking,' she admits. 'Previously I'd watched all the other contributors dash around, and helped them get their material together – sometimes at the last minute – but this time it was all down to me. Even when I'd produced the copy and got the photos I wanted, I was still very nervous that the editor would not like it. In the event, she was very happy with it.'

Since the magazine is put together by a team of six people, when the assistant fashion editor left, Shona was the obvious candidate to take over the job. While it was a considerable step up in terms of her own responsibility and required more editing and day-to-day management skills than creativity, she found the job extremely enjoyable. She is now hoping to find an editorial post on a national lifestyle magazine: 'It can seem that there are very few opportunities when you reach editorial level in magazines,' she admits, 'and competition for the positions which do emerge is extremely fierce. But I think once you've built up a strong reputation in the area, people know what you can do and will appoint you on the strength of that.'

5 Transmission: TV and radio journalism

The past few years have seen the expansion of broadcasting through local and independent radio, a new terrestrial channel, satellite TV and the continuing expansion of the cable network. The number of broadcasting organisations will continue to grow in the future, especially with the advent of digital broadcasting set to boost the number of TV channels available to every household into three figures.

More detailed information on working in broadcasting is given in *Careers in Television and Radio* (Kogan Page) but it should be noted than the expanding TV network will not automatically mean more opportunities for journalists in TV. Indeed, it is likely that most channels – if they carry the news at all – will take a news service from an independent provider rather than supporting their own news rooms. ITN, Independent Radio News and even the Teletext services are current examples of news organisations who provide such a service. It should also be noted that there will always be fierce competition for jobs within this sector, however many news rooms are established.

What skills do you need?

There is no standard route into broadcast journalism. Many of the current newscasters and editors worked in print media before entering the TV or radio studio. While these journalists must have good presentation skills – a good speaking voice and televisual appearance – they still need to be able to find the heart of a story and write about it in an engaging and informative manner. It is worth noting, however, that the nature of the medium affects both the style and content of a news report.

A news broadcast may last for only 30 minutes, a bulletin may last 60 seconds. While a newspaper reader can decide which order to read the newspaper and decide whether or not to read parts of less interest, broadcast news editors and newscasters must decide which stories will grab the audience's attention, how much time can be devoted to each item and how the item should be presented. Recently, presentation appears to have become more important than the news content itself. The cable channel L!ve TV has come in for much criticism for using 'news bunny' – someone dressed in a rabbit costume reacting to news stories in mime. Channel 5's news service was promoted through its revolutionary presentation style which dispensed with the traditional news desk as much as through the quality of its reporting.

In essence, radio and TV offer more immediacy than newspapers. Rather than working to an evening deadline for tomorrow's paper, journalists will work all through the day to provide material for a series of bulletins. In addition, journalists may deliver news live, reporting dramatic events like the Gulf War as they happen, or from significant locations such as the Houses of Parliament or the scene of a crime. The medium allows viewers and listeners to get the feeling they are 'on the spot', following stories as they develop rather than reading about them after the event.

Reporting live from these scenes without being able to edit in any way requires special skill. The reporter has to comment off the cuff, and keep that commentary going. There is no time to give much consideration to framing the actual words; no opportunity to cut or rephrase. Once at the location of the incident, the reporter has to assess the situation, keep the talk going, and even seek interviews or comments from the public or officials who are around the scene.

Since many reports will go out live, journalists have to work to very strict deadlines and with strict timing. They may have less than an hour to write a report, edit and script it and ensure the report lasts precisely 2 minutes and 30 seconds. The same demands may be made on prerecorded material, whether radio or television, so that the programme producers know how long each item is going to last.

Reporters are dispatched by a news editor to cover a story which may have come from contacts with local people, such as the police or local freelance journalists, known as 'stringers'. Some items may come from news agencies and others are diary events already on the calendar, such as royal visits or sports meetings.

The television reporter will be part of a team that includes a technical crew of camera operator, sound technician and lighting assistant.

It is up to the reporter to decide whom to interview at the scene of a story and how to present it. Notes are made about the content of the film, so that it can be edited back at the studio. Increasingly, this team of news gatherers is being cut back. Reporters may be sent out with only a cameraman for company, dealing with lighting and sound between them.

Case Study

Jake took the one year NCTJ journalism course at the London College of Printing having completed his first degree in sociology.

Jake had been an active journalist at college, contributing a wide range of articles to the campus newspaper each year and taking one year on sabbatical to edit the publication. While the experience had given him a firm grounding in journalistic techniques he felt he would benefit from a professional course and the recognition the qualification would give him.

The course was far ranging and taught him a lot about journalism law as well as allowing him to apply his skills to other media. He learnt how to use DAT (Digital Audio Tape) recorders and to edit together an audio news story. 'At first, I was so used to working in print I found putting across ideas and arguments in sound extremely difficult,' he says. 'We had to think about sound effects and location – where we wanted to be when we were giving the report – as well as the content of the report itself. With newspapers, you know your reader will be sitting down and concentrating on what you have written; with the radio, you have to learn how to grab the listeners' attention and keep them interested.'

As part of the course, Jake took work experience in the news room of a regional radio station. 'The rate at which news stories developed was incredible,' he says. 'You'd get half way through preparing a script for one story and then find the situation had changed or someone else had made a statement which your story had to include. Stories for the hourly bulletin were sometimes ready only minutes before broadcasting.'

Since leaving college, Jake has worked in both newspapers and radio. One tabloid paper sent him to 'doorstep' someone in the public eye. 'I didn't really enjoy doing that,' he admits. 'But sometimes you have to be persistent to get a good story. There were a few of us waiting to speak to this person and it was exciting to think that I could find out something which would make the front page the next day.'

Jake is sceptical about the future of the printed press and is worried that newspapers may become obsolete in the future, or at least decrease in readership to the extent that there will not be the opportunities and challenges that he wants from the job. For this reason, he is keen to maintain his links with both media and is considering further training which will help him find a position in a television newsroom. 'People want to know what is happening right now,' he says. 'They want to know, and the best way of doing that is through the radio or TV. Newspapers offer more in terms of analysis but not many people have the time to read them.'

Specialist jobs in TV and radio

In America, CNN (Cable Network News) has employed journalists as 'video reporters'. These reporters go to the scene of their stories on their own with a video camera. They shoot the material they require – using a tripod and remote microphones for interviews – and edit their own reports together back at the studio. While this may seem a near impossible task and a way of cutting back on CNN employees, it also gives the news reporter complete control over their material and how the story is put together.

Features or magazine-type reporting for radio and TV are usually more leisurely, and can be planned in advance. Many of these programmes are prerecorded and can therefore be shortened or edited before going out from the studio. While the same kind of reporting skills are needed, the pressures of immediacy are much less.

Just as on the newspapers, there are correspondents who cover either specialist subjects such as politics, crime and the arts, or who work permanently overseas, sending back reports on their areas. Special correspondents and investigative journalists may also contribute to or make full length documentary programmes covering issues, places or people in depth.

The most glamorous of the television jobs are those of the presenters, the people who read the news in the studio. Presenters are also known as anchor-men or women since it is their job to hold the programme together, introducing each item – whether prerecorded or live – and ensuring the show runs smoothly. While the presenter's script is pre-written there may be sudden developments or crises during the broadcast with which he or she has to cope. A story may suddenly break which means losing one item and switching to a completely different subject. Alternatively, an outside broadcast may be impossible to receive, leaving the presenter to fill in while the technical hitches are ironed out.

Journalists in this position are usually very experienced, will be thoroughly prepared for the programme, up to date with current news and familiar with each item they present. In this way, they will still be able to ad lib and keep the programme moving whatever problems arise.

Behind the cameras and microphones there is a great deal of research and writing to be done for all news and current affairs programmes. As well as the larger tasks of planning and preparing programmes and scheduling, the work includes editing and checking for accuracy, writing linking copy and trailers, devising maps, graphics and captions when necessary and scripting the news items.

Getting started

At present, there are probably fewer than 5,000 full-time broadcast journalists in the UK, including those working for the BBC, independent radio and television, satellite broadcasting and the specialist production companies, according to the National Council for the Training of Broadcast Journalists (NCTBJ). It is becoming increasingly desirable to have a degree, either in journalism, or in a subject such as politics, history or economics, which would be relevant to a future career. The next step is a place on a company training scheme or an NCTBJ-recognised course in broadcast journalism.

Some journalists who are taken on to work in radio and television will have had many years' experience of working for a newspaper as a reporter or sub-editor and already have the NCTJ National Certificate. Most new recruits to radio and television take an NCTBJ-recognised pre-entry course. Although courses in broadcast journalism concentrate on teaching radio journalism skills, they should all have components on television work. Students are trained as bi-media journalists, enabling them to move between radio and television, and in some cases to work in both forms of broadcasting at the same time.

On spec applications are not likely to be as successful in radio as in newspapers. The BBC does not normally consider any that are not related to advertised vacancies. However, they do advise contacting the Programme Organiser of local radio stations if you have anything to offer as a freelance or contributor. Staff of BBC local radio are recruited through BBC Corporate Recruitment Services in London.

Vacancies are advertised in the *UK Press Gazette*, *Broadcast* and the *Guardian* media page (Mondays) and on CEEFAX or, occasionally, in the case of local stations, in the provincial press. Many full-time journalists got their first job as a result of the contacts they made on their pre-entry course. Most courses include a period of work experience at a local radio or television station and this can be invaluable. Because broadcasting is so immediate and time-conscious, news editors need people who can do the job the moment they enter the studio. Any radio experience, such as helping with a university or hospital radio, or contributing items to a local radio station, will help in getting a job. At national or major station level, someone who has experience in local radio will have an advantage over someone with purely newspaper experience.

Case Study

James *went into the Army as a young man and, after training, went overseas, attached to a signals unit, as a wireless operator. Here he used portable equipment for transmission and receipt of messages and moved from place to place with the unit. At the end of his term of service he returned home to London, but not before he had had some small experience with broadcasting news and entertainment to the troops, as distinct from the strictly military transmissions which he had been doing before.*

James thought he might turn his experience of broadcasting equipment and programming to good use, and succeeded in getting a job in a local broadcasting station. By this time he had acquired some of his own portable recording apparatus and was itching to go out and report on something for the station. However, his work for the station was all indoors in the studios, although he did get the opportunity of seeing how they used their much more sophisticated technical equipment, how the programmes were planned, and how they were produced.

'I was writing and editing scripts for them, but I wanted to put forward suggestions of my own for programmes which I felt sure would get a good response from our listeners. The station authorities welcomed my ideas in principle, and asked me to submit more details. I did this, and waited. In due course, they came back to me and said that they would try out a pilot programme and see what response it brought. I had to put the pilot programme together myself, and eventually it went out. We then awaited listener response. I was a bit anxious, but the results were very satisfactory indeed – more letters and phone calls than even I had expected. So another programme was put together, and eventually it became a regular feature.'

James now spends much more of his time outside the studios, reporting, interviewing, attending meetings, press conferences etc, and still has his stint to do in the studio, so his work is a mixture of reporting, programming and editing. He could do similar programmes through the medium of television, but prefers to work as a radio journalist.

Wired writing: Internet publishing and new technology

If you've just returned from a desert island or only recently pulled your head out of a bucket of sand, you won't know what the Internet is. Basically, it's an information network between computers linked by the telephone system that allows individuals to access data and communicate with other computers – and therefore computer users – all over the world. To access the Internet you need a computer, a telephone, a modem (which sends and receives computer code down the telephone line) and an Internet Access Provider (IAP) who connects your phone line to the rest of the computer network or World Wide Web. Most IAPs charge for their services by the month and give you free software to enable you to navigate the web with your computer.

Accessing the Net

In order to find the information you want, you need to know the appropriate website address – also known as Uniform Resource Locator or URL for short. URLs begin with http://www. followed by further text which tells the navigating programme where to look for the information. A URL will specify the country, location and computer where the information is held. There are also special 'search engines' on the net which will search through directories of web pages matching pages to a single word or group of words you submit. Search engines are useful because they can lead you to Internet pages of which you were previously unaware. Equally, they can produce long lists of pages which have nothing to do with your subject.

Once connected, further navigation can be carried out using the 'point and click' principle common to computer operating systems which have a mouse: simply point the arrow at what you want, click the mouse button and the IAP will connect you with that service. Users can therefore flick between web pages without typing in new URLs. This has become known as 'web-surfing'.

For any journalist, writer or copywriter, the Internet is a powerful tool well worth knowing about. It is also fairly simple technology to get to know. Even web page construction languages such as HTML (Hypertext Mark-up Language) are within most people's understanding. There are no obvious career or training structures in the Internet and thousands of training courses are available from straightforward introductions to using the net to complex programming languages. Many people are and will remain self-taught, making new discoveries of how the technology can work for them on an individual basis.

Case Study

Jane left school after her A-levels and joined the personnel department of a national manufacturing company. For two years she was given a number of administrative posts and in her spare time she attended a local college and took a short course on word-processing.

'At the time, I took the course because it was something I thought would be useful. I hadn't had much access to the machines at school and when they introduced them at work a lot of people were scared about what they could do.'

Her company was planning to reorganise the way it operated in order to introduce new standards of work and Jane found herself on a new team charged with communicating the changes throughout the diverse branches of the company. 'I was put in charge of editing the company newsletter,' she says. 'When I took over, it was black and white, and consisted of two A4 sized sheets. It carried stories about employees who had received long-time service awards, new services and goods the company was involved in and a message from the directors.'

Over the next 12 months, Jane completely revamped the publication, turning it into a colour magazine carrying interesting articles on subjects of general interest rather than purely from within the company. 'I realised very soon that I didn't have the skills necessary to do what I wanted to do,' explains Jane. 'I wanted to interview people within the company, get their ideas and present them in an entertaining way.' Jane took evening classes in shorthand and touch-typing, both of which enabled her to work more efficiently. She also enrolled on a creative writing course which gave her more confidence in writing copy each month.

It was while she was on one of these courses that she found out about the Internet. She discovered that some companies were now using the World Wide Web to distribute a 'virtual' newsletter within their own organisation. The technology meant employees could read the newsletter from the computers on their desks. Each employee could print out articles from the computer if he or she wished but, essentially, the move meant there would be no need to print or distribute hard copies across the country. Jane presented the idea to her team and was sponsored to be trained in HTML which would enable her to put the newsletter on to a web site.

'The newsletter site has become extremely popular,' she says. 'I can put stories and photographs on it and link some stories to other company information web sites. I can update it whenever I want to and readers can write back to me simply by clicking an icon on the screen. I get far more feedback about the articles than I ever did when it was simply printed.'

What equipment will you need?

Your computer needs to be an IBM-compatible PC or an Apple Mackintosh. Modem speeds are now going up to 54 kbps (one kbps = one thousand bytes of information transferred per second) although many Internet Access Providers still operate at a maximum of 33.6 kbps. If you're starting from scratch, you will need to spend a minimum of £800 to get the equipment you need and to sign up to an IAP. You may be able to halve this cost by buying secondhand, but make sure the computer processor is at least a 486 and has 8 Mb of RAM otherwise you will have problems connecting to the service.

Modems plug into domestic telephone lines. A dedicated phone line or ISDN (Integrated Standard Digital Network) connection provides even faster data transfer rates – up to 128 kbps. Naturally, this technology comes with a fairly large price tag and so is more likely to be used by companies than individuals. Even then, some telephone exchanges are not modern enough to allow this kind of communication to take place.

ISDN creates the possibility of sending pictures and video images from one place to another electronically. It also offers direct computer links which means that one computer can look at information held on another computer without any information being sent between them. An editor sitting in an office in one part of the world could look at the layout on the page of a magazine held on a computer somewhere else, ask for alterations to that layout and immediately see the changes. Technology is changing the way business is done and no business will be more affected than the written media.

There are numerous Internet Access Provider companies, all offering different services for your money. Many offer a free 'trial' giving you free access to their service for a limited period of time. Some may offer you your own free web page. Most will require your computer to dial up a local number in order to access the net – and it's worth checking that the local number applies nationwide since you will have to pay the phone company for the calls you make to the provider's service. Some companies also start charging connection fees to the World Wide Web if you go over a certain number of hours 'logged on'. In short, look out for the hidden extras and be sure to take the service which meets your requirements.

There are many Internet and computer magazines in your local newsagents which will give details of and review Internet Access Providers as well as giving sound advice on the hardware you should buy. Take note of reports from actual users, particularly if they experience problems with connecting times for IAPs. One of the biggest problems with the technology is that so many people are opening Internet accounts that the providers can't cope with the demand. As a result, you may find your dial up number engaged just when you want to log on. A useful introduction to the virtual world is possible through visiting one of the growing number of Cybercafés where you can hire a computer with an Internet connection for half an hour or more. Some cafés offer e-mail address accounts so you can collect messages and carry out research from their machines. Universities and libraries may also have facilities you can use.

Why journalists need the Internet

The World Wide Web has proved important to the work of journalists in two ways. First, the Internet represents one of the biggest and most detailed research sources anyone could wish for. The main news providers, such as Reuters and Associated Press, have information here which is continually updated. National newspapers have direct connections with these press agencies in order to be aware of worldwide events as they happen. There is no quicker way to find out what is happening in the world.

At the same time, because of the diversity and number of people who are connected to the web, it is possible to find extremely obscure information or material which may not exist anywhere else. You can call up any number of pages generated by individuals and organisations around the world. There are personalised home-pages telling you about the interests of the authors, where they live and what they do – a sort of electronic pen-pal advert. There are complex web pages from academic organisations which feature research and catalogue completed projects offering data which would take months to locate and receive via land mail.

There is a website for any and every special interest group world-wide. One URL may take you to the website of Star Trek, holding information on every programme ever produced, plus an electronic forum where fans can 'talk' to each other via their computers. There are sites for everything from gardening to flying, the supernatural to the mundane. In theory, a journalist in search of a breaking news story can find it on the web, carry out in-depth research, even find and interview individual case studies without moving from the computer terminal.

Having written the article, the author can e-mail it directly to the editor's computer. This method means the editor does not need to re-input the article before manipulating it and putting it on to the page layout. In some cases, the first time a piece of writing becomes hard copy is when it is published in the final magazine.

Technology has increased the speed of business communications and opened up a new medium for promoters and public relations work. Rather than taking out advertisements or sending numerous press releases, businesses now have web pages which give details of their products and services, key personnel and even job vacancies. The ability to work with both the Internet and CD-ROMs is increasingly important for PR and publicity writers. Many freelance journalists are using similar skills to create their own web presence and sell their own news stories directly to web-surfing editors.

Another important issue for all journalists with regard to the Internet is that of putting material on the web. Many newspapers and magazines have web pages which include features, pictures, archive material and further information supplementing the publication. In some cases, staff are employed purely to write and edit material for the publication's website. Since the technology is still relatively new, there are still many avenues to be explored and many issues to be resolved – see especially the issue of copyright, mentioned in the next chapter on freelancing.

It is therefore in every journalist's interest to get to know the workings of the web. You do not necessarily need to understand how it all works, but you should have a clear idea of what it can do. There are many journalists who now make a lucrative living from writing purely about applications and advances on the Web, as well as those who are involved in designing web pages for publications and businesses.

CD-ROMs

The CD-ROM represents another area of technology of which journalists and writers should be aware. CD-ROMs can store incredible amounts of picture and text information on CDs which users can then access through their computer. These are thought to be the first versions of 'electronic books'. There is much discussion over whether CD-ROMs will eventually replace all printed media, but journalists should be aware of the medium as a research tool as well as a prospective market. CD-ROMs are frequently given away with computer magazines – and sometimes with magazines on other subjects. Knowledge of how CDs work and even how to write a CD would put a journalist at a great advantage.

Future developments

As the technology progresses, the possibilities will grow. It is uncertain quite how this technology will affect journalism in the long run. Suggestions that magazines and newspapers will become obsolete are somewhat exaggerated since the printed medium will always retain its own popularity and purpose. The proliferation of paper-based computer and Internet magazines surely proves this – some kind of information is best presented on the page. The cost of the technology is also prohibitive: not everyone can afford a PC and it would therefore be a mistake to publish only in an electronic medium. At the same time, predicting what the technology will be able to do in 10 or 20 years' time is impossible, so there may yet be new media which journalists will be needed to work on.

If you've already got the system set up, you will find all daily newspapers have a World Wide Web presence and carry their URL in the paper issues. In addition, the search engine Yahoo has a separate search engine for newspapers, magazines, TV and radio programmes.

Connect to http://www.yahoo.com. and explore from there. There are also excellent guide books to the Internet which include listings and tips for navigation, such as the *Rough Guide to the Internet* (Penguin). Internet magazines will also carry details of useful pages as well as reviewing the more important and intriguing places to visit.

Case Study

Nick *is the managing director of a publishing company that specialises in magazines for computer buyers. He graduated from Birmingham University with a degree in Economics seven years ago. The course gave him the background he needed to set up his own business, but his interest in technology proved to be the key to his career.*

'When I graduated, the market for personal computers was just developing. I identified a gap in the market place for a consumer magazine which would explain what computers could do for first-time buyers.'

Using his own computer and the services of a local printer, he produced a few dummy copies of his magazine. He used these to get the interest of advertisers and to secure a loan from the bank to start up the company. The first issues were produced by Nick and a friend, who shared responsibilities for writing copy, designing the pages and securing advertising.

Not only had Nick identified a strong demand from readers, but he also tapped into a lucrative advertising market. Many new retail and service companies were keen to use the magazine's pages to present their products to an interested and new audience. 'What made the magazine so successful was the quality of the writing,' says Nick. 'The first few issues were extremely hard work because we had to produce copy which would not confuse people who were new to the area while at the same time convince advertisers that readers would understand their products.'

Within a few months the company had expanded to a staff of five, and Nick was able to start a second title, targeted at small businesses. 'Qualifications in journalism were not first on my list when I was looking for staff to work on the magazines,' he explains. 'What I needed were people who knew the subject inside out. In any case, if you know about computers or have worked with them in any capacity, you will be able to use a keyboard. I taught myself how to use the applications we use – QuarkXPress, Photoshop and so on – but I would say that knowledge and experience in those areas are more useful to publishing magazines than touch-typing or shorthand.'

While Nick enjoys the business side of the operation – gaining new advertisers and launching new products – he maintains that publishing is an exciting and stimulating workplace. 'Working for the magazine — and for any magazine — means you are in touch with new developments as they happen. You get to review new products as they appear and talk to people who are at the cutting edge of the industry. The magazines are successful because they tell the readers what will happen in the future, and that puts the writers who work here in a very exciting position.'

7 Lone scribe: freelancing

Working as a freelance journalist means finding a market for your own writing. This can be done through:

(a) supplying, by previous agreed arrangement as to length of the article, item, story etc for an agreed rate of payment, a single contribution or series of contributions to a paper or magazine;

(b) writing a story, article or feature and then seeking to place it with a suitable publisher;

(c) becoming a regular correspondent for a publication, reporting local items in your own district;

(d) supplying on a regular or intermittent basis, for agreed rates of payment, specialist articles on hobbies, crafts, trade and business matters, the arts, medical subjects etc.

A freelance journalist does not need to have any particular educational qualifications, belong to any union or trade association, have any journalistic certificates or have done any apprenticeship. Clearly, as with all journalists, good use of English and the ability to write interesting copy are essential. Unlike other journalists, however, freelances must constantly find markets for their work and sell their ideas to editors as well as producing copy on time.

Freelance reporters usually have arrangements with newspapers or other media. They may not publish all the material the freelance produces but they will still pay 'retainers' to be kept in the picture about a certain issue or geographical location. Freelances can please themselves about their hours as long as they submit copy when the editor wants it, but here again, unless they are writing about regular events, they will be subject to the same unsociable hours as any other reporter.

Some freelances make a very good living and enjoy the freedom which self-employment gives them. But if you are depending on method (b) above, there is an element of insecurity, particularly if you limit yourself to just one or two publications which might then fold. Most freelances try to get a certain amount of regular work by the other methods listed above, which become their bread and butter, leaving the work under (b) to be indulged in as an extra.

Feature writing

The majority of freelance writers are feature writers. These are the articles which pick up current stories and study them in further depth. They may profile someone in the public eye or analyse the issues behind the headlines. Feature writing is particularly suitable for special-interest publications and many freelances move into this area of writing having worked in a specific area within industry or as a full-time reporter in that area for a publication.

It is essential to study the market. The best way of doing this is to look in detail at the various papers, magazines and books available for which you feel qualified to write. It is no good, for example, offering an article on wood-carving to the *Metals Bulletin*, or a feature on sewing machines to a magazine devoted to motor-cycling. Study the publications to which you intend to submit material before you start writing anything. You need to know the magazine's style of writing, and what is being published now, in order to assess what might be acceptable in the future.

Case Study

Dave *is a freelance writer working from home in a northern town. He did a three year journalism course and worked for two years as a local reporter on the area's main newspaper.*

'There was a lot of talk of redundancies while I was there,' he explains, 'and while I enjoyed the work, I was never sure how long I would be employed for.'

In fact, Dave decided to go freelance before the paper could try to make him redundant. 'It wasn't an easy choice to make,' he says, 'and there have been times when I wonder if I did do the right thing, but I wouldn't go back on it now.'

While Dave was working on the press, he was able to build up contacts with many people from the local media. He found the same faces would appear at press launches and events and soon he had built up a large circle of acquaintances. When he went freelance, he made sure all these people knew of his decision. The paper he left was still interested in receiving work from him, but so too were the other local publications. On occasions, Dave found he could cover the same basic story for both the daily newspaper and the weekly listing magazine. All he needed to do was to find a different angle for each case and both clients would be happy.

With extensive knowledge of the area, Dave also wrote to a number of regional editors on the national papers. He offered them a few stories giving a local angle on a subject which the dailies could not possibly achieve from their London base. Occasionally, the national editors would phone him up to see if he would cover an issue in his area for the paper. 'I'm on the mailing list of all the local PR agencies and so receive loads of press releases every day. These may vary from a visiting celebrity to a press night at the cinema to a new initiative from a local company,' explains Dave. 'I may not be able to use these stories immediately, but sometimes I can mix a number of them and create an interesting story that is suitable for a national paper or magazine.'

Dave is not under contract to any of his employers and has no real guarantee that his work will be used, but because he has built up a good reputation and a diverse base of clients, he can be sure of selling some work each week.

Approaching a publisher

Having identified the magazine you wish to write for, a quick phone call to the editor of the publication or newspaper section will establish whether they are open to articles from freelances. Some publications are written completely by in-house staff or by a set list of freelances. In addition, you will be able to find out whether you need to submit the whole article up front or whether you can send in a précis.

This information can also be found in the *Writers' and Artists' Yearbook*, published annually by A & C Black. The book shows clearly and concisely what magazines and papers require from contributors, freelance and otherwise. Details are given of the type of article, story or feature the publication uses, the approximate number of words which these contributions should contain, the rate of payment (usually per thousand words) and whether payment is made by prior agreement, on acceptance, on publication or at a certain fixed time following publication.

Current rates of payment are given wherever possible, and certain other information, such as whether photographs should accompany the article and whether or not a preliminary letter to the editor is required. Whether the book contains all the information you need or not, it is still worth giving a particular publication a call or sending a letter of enquiry to the editor since editors and editorial policy can change overnight.

If a large amount of work is involved in the writing of an article, or substantial expenses are incurred while researching it, it is advisable in your own interests to write a preliminary letter to a prospective publisher before embarking on the work. Also, unless you are contributing regularly to a publication, it is advisable to enclose a stamped, addressed envelope when sending off freelance contributions since some editors will simply bin anything they don't use. Sending a letter of enquiry or a piece which pitches your idea means you will not waste time writing an article nobody wants. It may be a subject which another writer is already covering in the next issue. Alternatively, the editor may have views on how the article should be written and the issues it should address and will want to discuss the piece before you start writing.

One danger of sending ideas alone to publications is that your ideas may find their way to in-house staff or other freelance writers. This is an unavoidable pitfall. While you have copyright on your written work, you cannot copyright an idea. For this reason, successful pitches must explain why only you can write this piece – it may be due to the relevant contacts you have, your unique experience or understanding. Travel writing is a good example of this – only you will have visited certain locations during a round-the-world trip or had certain experiences. (Perhaps this is precisely the reason why travel writing is one of the most popular areas of freelance writing and is extremely competitive.)

It is unlikely that an editor will commission a piece of work from a complete unknown. A new freelance writer will have to give some proof of ability. This usually means cuttings from past publications – even examples from school magazines will be suitable for a young freelancer – but if there are no examples to give, most editors will look at unpublished work to give them an idea of the writer's skill.

Once you have caught the interest of an editor, it is essential that you agree the terms and conditions for writing the article. This includes length (number of words), deadline for submission, how the text will be submitted (increasingly via e-mail or at least on computer disk with hard copy attached), accompanying pictures and, of course, how much you will be paid and when you will be paid. When you have agreed these over the phone, put the agreement in writing and send it to the editor who has commissioned the article from you.

This may seem overcomplicated, but it is too easy to forget these details, especially when flushed with the success of having your idea taken up and receiving a commission for the article. The problem is, if these details are not made clear or written down then you, the writer, will have no claim to remuneration and no control over how your work is treated. Agreements by phone are binding but written details will give you more control of your work. Some publications view freelance writers as a cheap way of securing copy and seem to take the attitude that seeing the work in print is reward enough. If you are to establish yourself as a freelance, you must go about the work in a business-like manner so editors know they can trust you to deliver copy and know they must pay you to do so.

Copyright issues

The Internet has presented a difficult issue for freelances concerning *copyright* of their material. When a freelance sells a piece of work, he or she sells the paper the rights to publish that article once only in the UK. If the paper wants to reprint the article, if another publication prints the same article, or if the paper prints it in an international publication, the writer is due another payment. Publishers are now trying to buy all rights from freelances for the work they do so that they can publish the work anywhere without having to pay the writer again.

The move has been precipitated by the growth in electronic publishing. A web page for a publisher can be a useful source of revenue while also advertising the publication itself. Naturally, if publishers can avoid paying for the material on those pages, the exercise becomes even more of a money-spinner. In addition, 'all rights' includes media that have yet to be invented. This means that if another electronic format emerges, the publisher can republish a freelance's work, take the money from selling the format and not pay the contributor at all.

When negotiating the terms and conditions for your work as mentioned above, be sure you are clear which rights you are selling. You can sell all your rights if you want to, but make sure the publisher pays extra for them.

Making a living

Freelances can make money out of one single idea by selling the article to different publications. You cannot sell precisely the same piece but you may be able to take a single idea and sell alternative angles to different editors. Freelances are finding their way into all media – contributing to TV and radio programmes, working for press agencies and advertisers. One subject or idea may be sold across different media.

Extremely successful freelances usually fall into the 'celebrity journalist' category. They may have worked their way through the industry and now have sufficient status to command substantial fees for contributions or columns. Alternatively, they may be specialists in a certain area – entertainment or business, for example. Freelance writing may simply be a 'second job'.

Indeed, many freelances do have secondary activities which help alleviate the financial uncertainty that accompanies the freelance lifestyle. It is certainly possible to make a living out of freelancing but it is difficult to do so from scratch – primary experience in the industry is extremely useful, both to understand how the industry works on a day-to-day basis and to establish some useful contacts.

There are many people who would like to think of themselves as writers but some mistake the desire to write with the ability to make a living out of the activity. There are a number of correspondence courses and clubs which support freelance writers. Some of their claims for success seem fantastic and you should always research organisations before signing up. Many of them address an older age group – those who wish to take up writing on retirement, for example.

It is worthwhile watching the trade papers – *UK Press Gazette*, *Media Week* and *Campaign*, for instance – which sometimes contain advertisements offering work to freelance contributors.

Case Study

Arthur was a freelance writer for some years before taking a permanent, full-time writing job with a large publishing house. The firm produced around 15 magazines, some weekly, some monthly, on a wide range of subjects from gardening to holidays and leisure subjects. Arthur worked mainly for one magazine, occasionally assisting on one or two of the others. Although his duties were to write and sub-edit, he was concerned mostly with the advertising side of the magazines.

'I found myself more and more involved with our advertising copy, whereas I would much rather have been writing features. The advertising side was growing rapidly, which was a good thing for the firm, who were increasing their circulation by leaps and bounds.

As well as the larger advertisers, we had a number of small businesses which gave us advertising but were not large enough to employ copywriters and didn't use agencies. This involved quite a bit of telephone contact with them, helping them to draft their ads so as to make the best use of the space they were taking, and convey their sales message tellingly to our readers. Sometimes they wanted help with illustrations, photographic work and captions too.

We started a free service to readers, who would write in asking us about certain products, where they could be obtained, and what our advice was about certain trade or business problems. The most interesting and informative of these queries (and the answers) were printed in the magazine. This brought us into contact with more and more suppliers and others in various trades which, in turn, led to more advertising, though that wasn't the prime object of our advice column.

The advertising became so successful that I became assistant advertising manager, but although it was promotion, it meant that I was doing hardly any writing at all.

Eventually, I decided to return to freelance writing. While I was debating the possible financial risk, I heard about a society which had decided to recruit a small professional staff to run a magazine for its worldwide membership. I contacted them at once as I was particularly interested in this society, went to work for them full time, and now, happily, edit the magazine myself! I am still able to do freelance work outside, which makes up the financial difference between my present job and what I would now be getting had I remained with my previous firm.'

8 Have pen, will write: other opportunities and related professions

Free newspapers

There are thousands of free papers nationwide. Some are nothing more than advertising sheets, with a very small amount of editorial matter included. Even so, there are opportunities here to learn sub-editing skills and layout techniques. This level of journalism is not to be scoffed at since it is both a lucrative area of publishing and an excellent training ground.

Free papers can often be the main alternative to the dominant local paper and will therefore cover stories overlooked by other publications. A few have training schemes but they are more likely to offer work experience or even a job to a newcomer to the industry than a priced paper.

The National Council for the Training of Journalist (NCTJ) has approved some free newspapers for admittance to the newspaper training scheme, depending mainly on the extent of editorial news coverage and on how far the newspaper is prepared to take part in training. If you do have the chance to work on a free newspaper, make sure the NCTJ will accept its trainees for registration.

Press agencies

Press agencies provide a wide range of services. They may collect and supply press cuttings and photographs for organisations and publications, they may provide an ongoing news service and they may undertake reporting tasks. They employ journalists, feature writers, photojournalists and others to provide these services. Most countries have a press agency located in a capital or provincial town providing a service either locally or on a national or international basis. Some are specialist, providing coverage, for example, on specific subjects such as agriculture, aeronautics or politics. Press agencies give indentured training in the same way as newspapers. News agencies such as Reuters and Extel Financial are particularly concerned with financial news, but there is also a service – World Entertainment Network News – that provides rock music and entertainment stories for radio and newspapers.

Jobs overseas

This book is mainly concerned with opportunities in this country, but if you read the professional press – such as *Campaign*, *Media Week* or *UK Press Gazette* – you will sometimes find advertisements for reporters and editors to serve in other countries. Some of these vacancies are for English-language papers, but most candidates will require a knowledge of at least one other language. The posts may be for a fixed term, probably not less than three years, or they may be on a permanent basis. Vacancies sometimes appear in the national dailies, as well as being advertised in the professional press.

These overseas posts frequently offer accommodation and fringe benefits, particularly in countries in the Middle East and the developing world. There may be tax-free salaries, education allowances, paid passage home for holidays, gratuities or pensions. The rates of pay are usually very good – they have to be in order to attract the kind of person that country wants – and sufficient to entice a journalist to leave the home country for some time, or even for good. Conditions of service vary throughout the world, as do the qualifications and educational standards required.

Many call for specialist writers – those with skills in subjects such as engineering, science, medicine, new technology, or education; some require radio journalists, press or public relations personnel.

If you do find yourself living and working in a different country for a substantial length of time, you should seek the advice of the Department of Social Security (DSS) in order to be clear about your rights as a UK citizen. While some workers have returned home because the climate of the new country didn't suit them, others have been sent home for 'political' reasons – not all the world has a free press. Others have returned home because the new country has a conscription scheme for the armed forces, for which immigrants are also liable.

Foreign correspondents are fewer on the ground than they used to be. In these days of Concorde and Jumbo jets, most papers find it cheaper to send reporters on short-term foreign assignments, paying the hotel bills and then bringing them back, rather than supporting them abroad permanently. Nowadays, the only resident correspondents normally found abroad belong to the big news agencies and broadcasting networks plus a handful of papers like *The Times* and major American papers.

There are a number of 'local hire' people, individuals who have made their own way abroad and try to make a living once they get there. This is far from easy. While there may be a few publications who will take individuals on as part-time correspondents or on an occasional basis, establishing a long-distance working relationship with a major newspaper in the UK is extremely difficult. In truth, the greatest opportunities exist in trouble spots where the need for copy is high and the cost of keeping resident correspondents on the scene prohibitive. A local hire can work for several organisations at the same time and can make quite a good living out of it – but it is not a way of life in which success can be relied upon and it depends on the individual being able to live comfortably in the area.

Press photography

Those who want to become press photographers can undertake training on a regional or local newspaper in exactly the same way as reporters. Similarly, freelance photographers may work for a number of publications, being employed to collect photos for a specific project or receiving payment per photograph.

They cover all the local events, from fêtes to royal visits, and if they progress to a national newspaper they can become involved in recording major national events and even war. A press photographer will also need to gather and write down information about the events connected with his or her pictures, so that a sub-editor will be able to write an accurate caption from what is supplied.

Press and public relations officers (PRs)

Public relations is a field which has expanded enormously during the last few decades. Nearly every firm has its own press officer or has an account with a PR agency who will look after the corporate image of that company in the media. PR is not the preserve of commercial companies since positions also exist in local and national government as well as other public bodies, charities, trade and social associations.

PR staff liaise with the press (national, local, magazines), radio and TV, with the firm's customers if a commercial undertaking, or with the members of the public if a charity or other kind of organisation. They answer queries, issue press releases and arrange promotional events – from mounting exhibitions and press conferences, to attending trade fairs, to writing brochures, contributing to house magazines, researching (for instance, surveying press cuttings for what is being said about the products of the firm, or the activities of the organisation), writing letters to the press, and perhaps some public speaking.

This part of the information industry is particularly suited to journalists. Successful PR people need to be able to communicate with the media in a concise yet informative way. If the aim of PR is to get coverage of a company or client in the national press then the PR officer must have some idea of how the media work and what kind of stories are suited to which publication.

Job specifications nowadays call for people with a good command of English and an ability to use it in writing 'clean, crisp copy' – essential qualifications for a journalist. It is possible to get into public relations without any journalistic experience, for example through a marketing position or a marketing course, but you will still need to demonstrate a strong writing ability. Many people get into public relations via a secretarial job: after learning the ropes as a secretary in a press office for a year or so, you are in a good position to apply for the next vacancy.

If you are interested in a career in public relations, you can contact the Institute of Public Relations for the names of practitioners who are happy to give careers counselling. Send a CV and a covering letter explaining your reasons for applying, and the Institute will send you a counsellor's name and address. They will also send you details of their monthly journal, *Public Relations*. Another useful journal is *PR Week*, published by Haymarket Marketing Publications. Jobs in PR and advertising are advertised in the appointments page of *Campaign* – the advertising industry's paper – as well as *PR Week*, for the PR industry, and the *Guardian* media pages, published on Mondays.

Government press services

The Stationery Office publishes official reports, books and magazines, prepared within the various government departments and ministries by members of the Government Information Service (GIS).

There are around 1,300 media experts in the GIS with the role of explaining government policy and actions to the general public. Most are based in London, but there are GIS jobs nationwide. One of the largest departments is the Central Office of Information, employing over 300 information specialists. They are involved in the production or commissioning of publicity material, leaflets and journals, and usually have had previous media experience in jobs such as journalism, photography, print buying, film production, marketing and exhibition design.

The output varies in content according to the department or ministry concerned, the subjects being as diverse as engineering and agriculture, environmental health and transport. There may be booklets and leaflets to write, posters to design, scripts for radio and TV to be produced, photographs to be captioned, material for exhibitions written up, advertising campaigns to be managed, information conveyed to the public. There may be house magazines to produce, telephone inquiries to deal with, and even some parliamentary work. Outside copy also comes in from freelance contributors and needs checking and editing.

Other departments with GIS staff include English Nature and the Countryside Council for Wales, the Natural History Museum and Building Research Establishment, as well as the Departments of Health, Transport, and Trade and Industry, and the Home Office.

These jobs carry Civil Service conditions. Sometimes they are advertised, or you can send in an application at any time, which will be kept on file.

Case Study

Jason *took communication studies at university. At first, he thought he wanted to go into PR but he spent one summer of work experience in a busy agency in London and decided the work was too stressful for him.*

'It was very exciting, but there was no way I could consider doing it every day of my life. I think the main problem I had was the emphasis on getting a client coverage in a national publication rather than simply presenting the client's story to the media.'

Uncertain of what to do having graduated, Jason took a part-time job helping out at a small book publisher's. Here he helped to organise mail-shots publicising newly published books and to co-ordinate launch parties. It was during such a launch party, celebrating local authors, that Jason met Diane, who worked for the Central Office of Information promoting the local area. Jason realised Diane's job was just what he was looking for.

'It just struck me out of the blue – public relations in this area means you are able to promote one area, get to know that subject really well and to help people who come to you. In the PR agency, we were constantly working to deadlines, working very hard to convince people that we had an interesting story to tell. Then, as soon as that deadline had passed, we moved on to a completely different subject or client. In the Information Office there was less pressure. You still had deadlines and needed to promote events happening in the area, but you were able to take a long-term view, build some really worthwhile relationships and generate real interest.'

Jason applied to the Civil Service and was taken on as an information officer within the Home Office. He was put on the fast-track training scheme and soon attained promotion. Today he runs a local information office.

Publicists

One of the specialised forms of journalism, linked to advertising, is the job of publicist. Advertising agencies and their staff are publicists by definition, but the term is often used in connection with journalists working for individuals or organisations whose objectives are not as wide as those of the advertising agencies.

A good example is the entertainment business. Actors, writers and musicians will either have a publicist working solely for them, or be part of a small group of clients for whom the publicist acts. The object, naturally, is to get their names before the public in the press and on radio or for them to be interviewed as a news item on TV, as distinct from the publicity which the performances themselves would get by way of a critic's write-up after the event.

This involves contacting the media before a performance and working up those contacts whether through meeting members of the press at theatrical venues, in studios, at press conferences, or social gatherings. The job requires an ability to write good, informative, but short and 'snappy' articles, paragraphs and news items, to arrange photography, write photographic captions, monitor press cuttings, give information over the telephone, arrange and attend interviews.

Jobs of this kind are likely to be advertised in papers such as *The Stage and Television Today*. In these columns will also be found advertisements for publicists at theatres and concert halls, the job here being similar to that of the publicist for individual artistes, but concerned also with writing handouts for circulation to firms, schools, clubs and social organisations or others on the theatre or concert hall's mailing list; helping to design or caption posters; writing up brochures or programme notes; arranging for and captioning photographs etc. The duties will probably include writing advance material for the press/radio.

Sometimes these jobs are advertised as being for a 'Marketing Assistant' or 'Marketing Manager', 'Publicity Assistant' or 'Publicity Manager'. Marketing manager in this respect should not be confused with the kind of marketing manager required to work on the accounts of advertising agencies.

Advertising

Advertising fluctuated during the recession, but it remains very big business. In an advertising agency, a writer works alongside an art director to create campaigns which bring together eye-catching images and words.

The art of advertising lies in the skilled use of English. The product message needs to be conveyed in as few, but as telling, words as possible. Besides sales literature, advertising copy, if effective, is extremely brief. Advertising messages can be slanted in several ways to make an impact. They may be humorous, make use of puns, alliteration or rhyme – every device in the English language and even sometimes deliberate misuse of it. A good 'punch line' should rivet the attention of the reader and immediately get across what the product, company, society or association has to offer.

Some firms employ advertising agents, while others have in-house staff. In the commercial field, the writer has to know the product or a number of products and what his or her customer – ie the advertiser – wants to get across, in general terms. In an agency, the firms for which the agency works will possibly change from time to time, so a new range of products will have to be written about.

The range of advertising channels for which copy is required is varied: outdoor posters, display advertisements in national, provincial and overseas newspapers and periodicals, air time on radio and screen time on commercial TV, mailing shots, handbills, brochures, advertising on packaging. It may include caption writing for films, or material for exhibitions. Sometimes longer copy is required, such as feature articles for the press in connection with particular campaigns, circular letters for mailing shots or sales brochures. There may be tight deadlines to keep if a particular campaign's news-worthiness is to have full effect, and in this respect the work of the copywriter is similar to that of the press officer.

Copywriting with a large organisation or with an advertising agency involves more than merely writing copy from simple directions. The copywriter must be a team player, working alongside artists, designers and production personnel.

The client – the firm or organisation paying for the advertising campaign – will have discussed with the agency management the message it wants to get across or the type of customers it wishes to address. There will be a financial budget for the campaign and discussions about the media to be used.

While the customer will not be involved at all stages of the campaign, there will be conferences about proposals and progress. There may be many attempts at a finished campaign before the final one is agreed. A campaign may switch media – from radio to television in order to capture a larger audience – and the copywriter will have to adapt ideas to suit as changes are made.

The success or otherwise of the team's efforts is evident from market research, feedback from clients and, ultimately, buyers.

Case Study

Sharon is promotions director for one of Europe's largest magazine publishing companies: Headway Home & Law Ltd.

'I went to a convent school which had a bias towards the arts, and achieved five O levels. This was followed by two years at business school to obtain an HND in Business Studies. Finally, I did evening courses and obtained a Diploma in Marketing.

I got into magazine publishing completely by accident. After a secretarial job or two, I moved into telephone sales, selling television air time. This led to Thames Television as a sales and marketing executive, followed by jobs abroad, and eventually on to a music paper as a sales and PR executive.

In my present job, I sell sponsored editorial features across 30 publications on subjects as varied as home interest, driving, and health and fitness; this involves making presentations within consumer and business companies, and writing detailed proposal documents with visual material.

The creative side involves devising ideas for clients which will meet their marketing objectives and capture their imagination. Once I have worked out the basic idea, I commission freelance designers, illustrators, photographers and writers to execute the project.

Management involves controlling all aspects of the project right through from the initial sales call to sending off the final copy. Two staff report to me.

I am paid a basic salary, plus commission; there is a private health scheme and I have a company car. I was fortunate enough to be head-hunted for this specialist job, which combines creativity and sales ability. The sheer variety is tremendously enjoyable; however, the pressure is severe – constantly meeting deadlines and targets. I would like to move more into a publishing role, or possibly be a creative director. I read all the newspapers and magazines and talk to people I know to keep aware of new opportunities.'

Winning writes:
top tips for getting into
journalism

Top Tips

for Becoming a Journalist

◆ Gain work experience in any way you can.
◆ Practice sub-editing – on anything you can lay your hands on!
◆ Practise your writing skills.
◆ Build up a portfolio of your work.
◆ Read as much as possible, particularly on your 'chosen' subject.
◆ Learn keyboard skills and shorthand – these are always useful.
◆ Learn computer skills – anything from word processing to DTP will stand you in good stead.
◆ Keep up with new technology – read about it and take every opportunity to get hands-on experience.
◆ Think long and hard about what you would like to write about, what interests you and what will continue to interest you in years to come.
◆ Make sure this is what you really want – the world of journalism is a competitive one, and you need to be assertive and pushy to succeed.

Gain work experience

Whatever area of journalism you decide to enter, you can make your first move into the industry much easier by getting work experience. If you are still at school you may be able to contribute to the school magazine. At college there will be a student orientated newspaper for which you can write and work. If there are no such publications, start one up for yourself. Many well respected journals started life in a small room with a photocopier. You may have to work for free initially, but any experience you gain will make you more employable.

Practise sub-editing

Naturally, your English course at school will give you an idea of how good your writing skills are and, more importantly, how much you enjoy using the English language. Look for projects which key into journalistic activities – paraphrasing and précis writing, for example. It is essential in journalism to be able to reduce copy to the length which a newspaper or magazine needs and to be able to do a certain amount of rewriting when required.

Try a few exercises at home: take a newspaper report of a lengthy speech and see how far it can be cut without losing any essential points. Take a rambling account of an event and see if the contents can be phrased in a more lively, readable style without losing any news value. To be able to do these things is good preparation for editorial work. Papers and magazines often receive contributions from people who are not writers by profession, and their manuscripts or typescripts have to be 'written up' or edited to make them acceptable to the readership. This process is known as 'subbing' (sub-editing) and has to be done carefully so as not to distort what the contributor has to say.

Practise your writing skills

Alternatively, your English course may ask you to write reviews and appraisals of events or books you have read. You may find you are particularly good at this area of work – able to assimilate the contents and style of a book very quickly and therefore to write a piece of constructive criticism on the subject. English essays which ask you to study aspects of a novel can be quite like book reviews, although these will tend to focus on one single element of the book rather than the entire read.

Build up a portfolio

You may consider writing letters to the press (especially your local paper) on subjects of local and national importance. As well as school magazines there are local news-sheets produced by churches, neighbourhood associations and other special interest societies. Be sure to keep a copy of everything you have published or work of which you are particularly proud. In this way, you can build up a portfolio of cuttings to show prospective employers. It is a good idea to keep copies in photocopy form since newsprint quickly fades. Many job advertisements ask applicants to submit cuttings – be sure when you do so that the cuttings you submit are relevant to the publication. Never send your only copy to an editor since you may never see it again.

Read as much as possible

Read – or simply look at – as many publications as possible. Pay attention to the length of articles the publication runs and any important elements of style. There is a very specific style, for example, to the 'human interest' articles which run in many magazines. You can learn a lot from studying the character, content, style and make-up of every publication you can lay your hands on. You will see how the current magazine market is moving in terms of style as well as content. A well-known author's advice to a hopeful new writer was to read as much of other people's work as possible, and the same is true for the prospective journalist.

Learn keyboard skills and shorthand

It is almost impossible to take a full-time position as a newspaper journalist without a knowledge of shorthand and typing. Some people in the profession have got by with 'two-finger', self-taught typing and their own particular brand of shorthand, but employers will not take seriously any applicant who does not have a reasonable typing speed and will look askance at any reporter who does not know how to write shorthand.

Full-time, part-time and evening classes in both shorthand and word-processing skills are available all over the country. You may be taken on as a trainee without them but you will be expected to learn them very quickly. Having them already would be a point in your favour. The skills are also useful from a practical point of view – touch-typing and shorthand will save a significant amount of time in collecting interview and research material, giving you more time to concentrate on writing the article itself.

In the case of provincial newspapers (including your local paper) it is almost mandatory to be able to take a good shorthand note using an approved, recognised system and, of course, to be able to type. Keyboard skills will be essential for magazine journalists too, though formal shorthand may not be essential, depending on the type of job you are going to do. Many journalists who work on magazines have no knowledge of shorthand, but their jobs are technical or specialist – dedicated to layout or production roles – and do not actually require such skills. Nevertheless, shorthand is an extremely useful accomplishment, and it is worth remembering that you may at some time want to move to a different type of job within the profession where shorthand is an absolute must.

Computer skills and new technology

Computer skills are also important in today's publishing world. Look through the job advertisements in any newspaper and you'll find magazines looking for writers and designers with experience of particular software packages. QuarkXPress, run on Apple Mac computers, has become an industry standard. This programme allows the user to arrange the layout of text and pictures in an effective way without having to commit anything to paper. There are many other desktop publishing (DTP) and design packages that will be helpful in the work place.

Journalists should also be aware of other ways in which technology can be used in their profession. Use of the Internet and e-mail is becoming crucial, while some publishing departments may rely on database programmes to share information and maintain news contacts.

Decide what you want to write about

You will find it easier to get into the profession if you identify the area which you want to write about and the type of publication you would like to contribute to. If you want to report on current affairs, make sure you keep well up to date so when you apply, you can demonstrate your knowledge and express your own opinions. You will never get a job working for a music magazine if you do not know who the current music stars are and when their new record is coming out.

Be assertive

It cannot be stressed enough how competitive the job market is in journalism and, in order to get the breaks you want, you will need to be assertive, put yourself forward and take advantage of the opportunities and projects available to you. At the same time, as this book has illustrated, there is a wide variety of work within journalism, so while one journalist may be concerned with writing sensational headlines and finding the next exposé, another may simply be involved in covering the machinations of one particular industry.

Consider futher education

Those who choose journalism as their prospective career may wonder whether it is worthwhile studying for a university degree, given that the industry requires specific workplace skills rather than intellectual ability. Over the last few years, the provincial press, the main training area, has increased its graduate recruitment to over 50 per cent of the intake. Editors generally do not ask for a degree as an essential prerequisite, unless they are looking for specialist writers, in which case a relevant degree subject will show you have the necessary knowledge to understand and write about that subject.

Graduates following courses approved by the National Council for the Training of Journalists as part of the provincial training scheme have less time to serve on training contracts than non-graduates. Some editors may advise potential entrants to go for a degree if they think they have a good chance of obtaining one, but there is no single answer to suit all cases. If a school leaver retains a practical outlook and good news aptitude, he or she may become an excellent journalist through becoming a graduate, but no one can predict this. Degrees are more likely to be asked for if you are entering the BBC journalist training schemes, the marketing and advertising fields, or the book trade.

Forward writing: the future of journalism

There has been much speculation as to the future of journalism, especially with the advent and incredible growth of the Internet. Suggestions that technology will ultimately replace the printed page may be exaggerated but nevertheless journalists must be ready to work with electronic publishing in the future.

This does not mean that the workplace will be populated by computer programmers. The main reason for techno-fear is that people do not understand how the technology works. The fact is you do not need to know how it works, you just need to know what it can do. Even if newspapers are replaced by electronic media, there will still be a need for journalists to create copy published on those media.

There is also a general feeling that society is becoming more visually orientated. Fewer people get their news from newspapers, preferring to see or hear events through the TV and radio. Again, the extent of this shift is difficult to assess but it does means that journalists must be prepared to work in a variety of media throughout their careers. This consideration has been incorporated into some degree and training courses. As with understanding technology, journalists need to know how best to use the media to get their story across and they still need the same basic skills to research and write their story in the first place.

Consumers have become far more knowledgeable about how the media works. They are aware of how images and arguments can be manipulated to tell one side of a story and consequently can be very sceptical about the news they are told. In addition, the number of sources to which people can turn for information and the speed with which people can access up-to-date information are growing. As the various media battle for the public's attention, it is becoming increasingly difficult to discern good news stories from attention-grabbing trivia.

Journalists must constantly find new ways of telling their stories so that their audience does not become complacent or disbelieving. The public's shock threshold has increased as global communications have brought strong images from around the world into every household – images of war, famine, disaster and greed. Many journalists have complained that the issues they are reporting are no longer taken seriously – either by the broadcasting organisations or by the public. It has been suggested that the public have become tired of these issues – the phrase 'compassion fatigue' was coined a few years ago – and journalists now must work hard to ensure that their stories are not passed over as just another example of inhumanity.

There seems to be more popularity today for voyeuristic articles and exposés of the rich and famous. Effective news reporting has become a matter of audience figures rather than bringing world events to the people.

Related to this, there has been a tendency for the media actually to create news stories and to dictate the issues, rather than report them. Politics is a particularly good example of this. A political speech may contain many different ideas and new material, but a reporter may address only one of those issues, concentrate on an old idea which appears to have been dropped or investigate an issue completely unrelated to the speech. The issue of 'sleaze' played an important part in the early stages of the last general election, and yet that issue gained prominence almost entirely through the interest of the press. This may be another example of concern for readership and audience figures taking precedence over news reporting.

There has also been talk of government interference with the liberty of the press. Politicians from all sides have raised questions about bias within the media and introducing measures to curb cheque-book journalism and press 'intrusions' into private lives. In the future, journalists will need to continue the fight for the freedom to report on subjects in the public interest. Alongside that, however, comes the obligation to maintain high standards and to ensure that the subjects they report on are in the public interest.

Many of today's newspapers and magazines are sold through the competitions and reader offers they carry. Magazines are extremely fashionable – indeed, to the point of becoming fashion accessories – attractive for the lifestyle they depict rather than for the information they carry. The fashion side of the industry has been a direct result of new technology which has enabled anyone to become a graphic designer and experiment with the appearance of a publication. As technology keeps moving forward, this aspect of the industry will continue to develop. There will be more opportunities for graphic designers as well as those who can combine design skills with excellent writing and editorial skills.

All of these influences are present in the industry but none will completely dictate the shape of the future for journalists. There will always be the more serious press and the tabloids; the frivolous 'And Finally' news items to leave the viewers happy about life in general; and the uncovering of war crimes or fraud. The reporting of world events has always been regarded as a public service as well as a commercial activity, but journalists entering the industry today have a duty to ensure this continues, fighting against the trivialisation of current affairs, providing accurate and up-to-date reporting and unbiased analysis.

11 Qualifications available

There are a mixture of vocational and academic courses available, ranging from evening classes in typing and shorthand to four-year sandwich degrees in communication studies. The key to success is identifying the qualifications you need for the position and the level at which you want to enter the industry.

Daily and provincial press trainees

Direct entrants to the industry via provincial newspapers must have at least five GCSE/SCE passes, including English language, though some newspapers may also require recruits to have one or two A-levels. These standards are only a guideline: some publications will demand more qualifications; others may accept equivalent qualifications or decide the applicant is qualified in other ways. New recruits can undertake in-house training or external training. Alternatively, new recruits may have already taken a relevant degree or pre-entry course before applying for the position.

Some papers sponsor recruits through their education and, in some cases, in-house courses can include NCTJ (National Council for the Training of Journalists) recognition. The NCTJ syllabus consists of use of language, shorthand, law (as affecting journalists and the press), public administration (local and central government) and practical journalism. Students will therefore be well versed in the technical and theoretical matter of publishing as well as having good practical skills such as shorthand and touch-typing.

Magazines and periodicals

There is no compulsory training scheme for magazine journalists but a regulated training system does exist, supervised by the Periodicals Training Council (PTC), under the auspices of the Periodical Publishers Association (PPA). The system which effectively sets training standards for the industry is based on National Vocational Qualifications in five key areas and trainees can gain S/NVQs in Periodical Journalism at Level 4 in: writing news, writing features, subbing, subbing with layout and periodical design. S/NVQs are a proof of competence, demonstrating that the student has the knowledge and skills to do the job. These S/NVQs will be based on workplace assessment of what the trainee can do. There is no limit to the length of time taken to qualify, but it normally takes under two years.

The PTC advises both school-leavers and graduates to try to get a place on a pre-entry course. A-levels are usually required and any additional experience, such as writing for the school/college magazine or local newspaper, will help with an application.

It is possible to start work on a magazine without any qualifications in periodical journalism and to receive training from the company you work for. Reed Business Publishing, Morgan-Grampian, IPC, EMAP and Haymarket all own a number of periodicals and are big enough to run in-house training schemes. Normally, entrants have a degree in a related subject but there are exceptions for some titles. In recent years, the number of entrants has been cut and it is worth contacting each company individually to check whether or not they are running their scheme this year.

As an example of what you can expect, Morgan-Grampian's editorial intensive trainee scheme lasts for ten months and their trainees are considered to be fully trained within two years. On-the-job training includes working on two or three different publications, combined with courses in keyboard skills, shorthand, news and feature writing, sub-editing and production, interview techniques and law and finance for journalists.

While EMAP's 20-week course is open mainly to company employees, there are a few places available for fee-paying students. Reed Business Publishing, on the other hand, offers a 13-week course which may lead to a three-month period of work experience and a job, although there are no guarantees.

Some shorter courses can also help towards getting editorial work. The PTC publishes a *Magazine Training Directory* which features courses run by six training agencies. Course titles include 'The Deputy Editor', 'Evaluating and Developing your Publication' and 'Motivation and Leadership'.

Principal examining bodies in commercial subjects

The London Chamber of Commerce and Industry examines in many commercial subjects at Levels 1, 2, 3 and 4, and issues its own certificates to successful candidates. The examinations include shorthand and typing at various speeds, and word-processing, each of which may be taken as single subjects, and also third-level Group Diploma in Public Relations. The examinations may be taken while still at school, or subsequently. Certain colleges (including Pitman's) prepare candidates specifically for these examinations.

Pitman

Pitman's Examinations Institute has its own examining body as well as running courses in preparation for the examinations of the London Chamber of Commerce and Industry and the Royal Society of Arts.

Pitman Training Ltd offer over 40 different courses using audio-visual and multi-media techniques and start any of them on any working day. They also run a Diploma Programme aimed at those wishing to develop a range of office skills. They are based at over 50 training centres and include training in computer applications, typewriting and Pitman 2000 shorthand.

Royal Society of Arts

The Royal Society of Arts examines in a number of subjects for the award of RSA certificates. These subjects include shorthand and typing at various speeds, and computer keyboard skills, and the examinations may be taken as single subjects. It is possible to sit for them while still at school, or subsequently. The level of examinations in commercial subjects runs from elementary to postgraduate. The RSA also administers the S/NVQs Level 4 in Periodical Journalism in conjunction with the Periodicals Training Council, and the S/NVQ Level 4 in Newspaper Journalism in conjunction with the National Council for the Training of Journalists. The Society is known throughout the world for its certificates and deals with more than three-quarters of a million candidates yearly. The syllabus may be obtained directly from the Society. It is also possible to obtain copies of past examination papers.

TV and radio

While some colleges and universities can now offer students the chance to work with professional equipment and simulations of the commercial environment, for a long time the only opportunity for TV or radio journalism existed with the BBC. As with all their training courses, there are a limited number of places each year and these places are always extremely over-subscribed.

The BBC runs two journalism training schemes: one regionally based, the other based in London. Both are advertised in summer and autumn in the national press and both are over-subscribed. The courses last about 18 months and are devoted to learning the techniques of reporting and interviewing, running a studio and producing radio programmes. Talks are given by outside speakers and senior BBC journalists. Trainees learn how to write to film and ENG (electronic news gathering) techniques, make their own reports and programmes. They are also trained in interviewing techniques for radio, news collection and selection, tape editing, writing for radio, law and public administration, local and national government as well as shorthand and typing. During the rest of the training period, trainees are sent to practise within the BBC.

The ITV newsroom employs journalists directly from the independent companies so all ITV training takes place within the regional, independent, programme companies. Formal training schemes exist for those with no previous experience in the press or radio. They normally begin in September and are advertised in the national press.

Although recruits do not necessarily need previous professional journalistic experience, they are expected to have a good class of degree in any discipline and a natural flair for writing news. Personality is equally important to successfully gaining a place on these courses. Recruits must be self-confident, have drive, maturity, and the ability to work as a member of a team and make quick decisions. As with all journalists, they need to be highly articulate and able to remain calm under pressure.

Qualifications and training for photographers

Minimum educational qualifications required for acceptance on to an NCTJ training scheme are the same as those for reporters. If you wish to enter the field directly without taking a pre-entry course, you need four GCSEs (A – C) including English. Candidates who do not have the required number of GCSE passes are still eligible if they have had at least two years' relevant experience of photographic work, not necessarily in the newspaper industry, or have taken an equivalent course of further education in photography.

Once recruited to a newspaper, a new entrant may be required to serve a probationary period of six months, followed by a period under a training contract. This may include two eight-week, block-release courses held at Sheffield College (Stradbroke Centre) where there are proper facilities for training photographers in a journalistic environment. A National Vocational Qualification (NVQ) in Newspaper Journalism (Press Photography) at Level 4, or a National Certificate in Press Photography will be awarded in many companies after successful work experience. Alternatively, you may decide to take a pre-entry course in press photography or photojournalism.

Press photographers in Scotland normally take a full-time course in photography at a college of further education in Glasgow or Edinburgh and then apply for work on a newspaper – but there are not many vacancies.

PR qualifications

The Communication, Advertising and Marketing Education Foundation Ltd (CAM) is the examining body for the advertising and public relations industry. CAM awards the CAM Certificate in Communication Studies, the CAM Diploma in Advertising (for those who work in advertising) and the CAM Diploma in Public Relations (for those in PR). You can study for these qualifications either full time or part time and, once again, there are other degree courses which cover the areas of PR and advertising.

Scottish Vocational Qualifications (SVQs) and National Vocational Qualifications (NVQs) are due to be introduced in the industry, based on assessments of knowledge (by examination) and competence (through observation at the place of work).

The Business and Technology Education Council (BTEC) and Scottish Vocational Education Council (SCOTVEC) examine for their own certificates and diplomas at varying levels in business studies, which can include shorthand and typing.

The BTEC Certificate and Diploma in Media aims to provide a foundation of basic skills relevant to broadcasting and other areas of the media industry. Option units include: Interview and Presentation Skills; Marketing and the Media; Print Editing; Print Origination and Production. Entry qualifications are: minimum age 16; BTEC First Certificate or Diploma in a relevant subject; four GCSE passes, grades A – C or an equivalent qualification; and courses can be full or part time.

The Direct Marketing Association (DMA) recognises diplomas and courses in marketing skills and press relations. Further details from: Direct Marketing Association, Haymarket House, 1 Oxendon Street, London SW1Y 4EE; 0171 321 2525.

Higher and further education

Many colleges now run media-orientated courses offering students practical experience of working in a newsroom or studio, on a paper or magazine as well as the theoretical side of the industry. Courses in communication studies and media studies offer a range of project and field work in all areas of the media, from local newspapers to mass media publications.

College resources or placements with local and national news organisations may be possible to give the student a flavour of different work environments, and individual college resources will determine to a great extent the possibilities open to students in that area. Students can therefore study the general area of news collection, writing and publishing without having to commit themselves to one specific medium. HND and degree courses often follow a modular structure which means that students can decide which area they study and how that study is carried out. In this way, students can get a background in the field and useful work experience. Having graduated, they may then decide which particular area to work in and can take further vocational training courses if necessary.

For graduates who have already taken a first degree, there are also postgraduate diplomas and vocational training courses which will open the door to working for the media. The Newspaper

Postgraduate Diploma at the University of Central Lancashire, for example, immediately gives students the experience of working under the pressure of today's electronic newsroom. There are also a number of European and International Media orientated postgraduate courses reflecting the globalisation of all media.

When selecting the course for you, make sure you find out what areas of the media you will be able to gain first-hand experience of, what links the college has with the professional industry, whether the course is recognised by the NCTJ and what specific professional skills the course will give you.

Other training

Typing and shorthand are skills which anyone can get at any time. School-leavers may be able to obtain such skills and even get a start in journalism through their local Training and Enterprise Council (TEC). In Scotland, similar training is given through Local Enterprise Councils. Training can be full time, part time, distance learning, and you can even buy tutorial material off the shelf in book form or computer-based training.

Fees are very reasonable, even though they have been increasing in recent times. Courses can last from three months to a year (depending on the frequency of lessons).

Speed-writing

This is a shorthand system using letters of the alphabet instead of symbols. The principle of the method is to abbreviate ordinary English words by cutting out some of the vowels, double consonants and so on. This means you can construct phrases and sentences from dictation and read them back easily.

It is possible to take a 'home' course in speed-writing from the London Business College. Booklets explain the methods, and included in the correspondence course are audio cassettes to give the necessary dictation practice at home. There are a number of schools throughout the country which teach the method in classes and it is possible to take an RSA or GCSE examination in the subject. The speed-writing system claims to be able to attain speeds of 100 wpm within two months.

Speed-writing would be of use only to freelance journalists and others who do not intend applying for NCTJ training, as it would not be acceptable for use in the Proficiency Test.

12 Where to study

Daily and provincial press training

Applicants to recognised, full-time courses should contact the **National Council for the Training of Journalists**, Latton Bush Centre, Southern Way, Harlow, Essex CM18 7BL enclosing a 9" x 4" SAE; 01279 430009

Magazine and periodical training

London College of Printing, School of Media, Herbal House, Back Hill, London EC1 5EN; 0171 514 6500

University of Westminster, School of Communication, 18–22 Riding House Street, London W1P 7PD, 0171 911 5000

Journalism Training Centre, Unit 8, Mill Green Road, Mitcham, Surrey CR4 4HT; 0181 640 3696

PMA Training, The Old Anchor, Church Street, Hemingford Grey, Cambridgeshire PE18 9DF; 01480 300653

Examining bodies

London Chamber of Commerce and Industry, Commercial Education Scheme, Marlowe House, Station Road, Sidcup, Kent DA15 7BJ; 0181 302 0261

Pitman Training Ltd, 154 Southampton Row, London WC1B 5AX; 0171 837 4522

Royal Society of Arts, 8 John Adam Street, London WC2N 6LY, 0171
930 5115

BBC

Regional News Trainee Scheme for Graduates and Local Radio Trainee
Reporter Scheme. Application forms are available from **BBC Corporate
Recruitment Services**, PO Box 7000, London W5 2WY; 0181 849 0849

ITV

A minimum of six months' experience in newspaper, radio or television
journalism is normally required for entry to the courses which are run by the
Training Department of the ITV Network Centre. Further information is
available from the Careers Information Service, ITV Network Centre, 200
Gray's Inn Road, London WC1X 8HF; 0171 843 8077

The industry training organisation for broadcast, film and video, Skillset, has
a free information pack. Contact: Skillset Careers Information, 124
Horseferry Road, London SW1P 2TX; 0171 306 8585

Independent short training courses in radio skills and techniques

Magnus Carter Associates, 1A Somerset Street, Kingsdown, Bristol BS2
9NB; 01272 244028

NMR Ltd, The Coach House, 2 North Road, West Bridgford,
Nottingham NG2 7NH; 0115 9817787

On Air Training, County Sound Radio, Chertsey Road, Woking, Surrey
GU21 5XY; 01483 451964

Advertising and public relations

The **Communication Advertising and Marketing Education Foundation (CAM)** offers a Certificate in Communication Studies and Diplomas in Advertising, and Public Relations. Institutes offering this include:

London Colleges

Cathy Ace & Associates, (for correspondence only) 106 Christchurch House, Christchurch Road, London SW2 3UD

Central London College, 213–215 Tottenham Court Road, W1 4US; 0171 636 2212

Lansdowne College, 7–9 Palace Gate, Kensington, W8 5LS; 0171 581 4866

Lewisham College, Tressilian Building, Lewisham Way, SE4 1UT; 0181 694 3215

London College of Further Education, 186 Clapham High Street, PO Box 481, SW4 7UG; 0171 498 4819

London College of Printing & Distributive Trades, 65 Davies Street, W1Y 2DA; 0171 514 6500

London Executive College, Bank Chambers, 313 Balham High Road, SW17 7BA; 0181 682 1011

London Guildhall University, 84 Moorgate, EC2M 6SQ; 0171 320 1000

Magdalen House Ltd, King's College, 522 Kings Road, SW10 0UA; 0171 376 5378

Martran College, 3 Nottingham Court, Covent Garden, WC2H 9AY; 0171 379 1032

ROI Communicators, correspondence courses only; 0181 767 4117

Outside London

Aberdeen College, Gallowgate Centre, Gallowgate, **Aberdeen** AB25 1BN; 01224 612000

Castlereagh College, Montgomery Road, **Belfast** B5 7BD; 01232 797144

Matthew Boulton College, Hope Street, **Birmingham** BT6 9JD, 0121 466 4545

Blackpool and The Fylde College, Ashfield Road, Bispham, **Blackpool**, Lancs FY2 0HB; 01253 352352

Bristol Business School, Coldharbour Lane, Frenchay Campus, **Bristol** BS16 1QY; 0117 965 6261

Chippenham College, Cocklebury Road, **Chippenham**, Wilts SN15 3QD; 01249 444501

Croydon Business School, Croydon College, Fairfield, **Croydon** CR9 1DX; 0181 760 5805

Stevenson College of Further Education, Bankhead Avenue, Sighthill, **Edinburgh** EH11 4DE; 0131 453 6161.

Central College of Commerce, 300 Cathedral Street, **Glasgow** G1 2TA; 0141 552 3941

Procum Associates, Henley on Thames, 25 St Andrew's Road, Henley on Thames, RG9 1HY; 01491 572086

YORACT, Trinity and All Saints College, **Leeds**; 01274 820444

Loughborough College, Radmoor, **Loughborough**, Leicestershire LE11 3BT; 01509 215831

Heatherington Associates, University of Northumbria, **Newcastle**; 0191 410 7250

Gwent College of Higher Education, Allt-Yr-Yn Avenue, **Newport**, Gwent NP9 5XA; 01633 432470

Highbury College, Faculty of Media & Community Education, Cosham, **Portsmouth** PO6 2SA; 01705 283287

Procum Associates, Reading College of Technology, **Reading**, *see* Henley on Thames for contact details.

Redhill Business School, East Surrey College, Claremont Road, Gatton Point, **Redhill**, Surrey RH1 2JX; 01737 770348

Rugby College of Further Education, Lower Hamilton Road, **Rugby**, Warks CV21 3QS; 01788 541666

SE Essex College of Arts & Technology, Carnarvon Road, **Southend on Sea**, Essex SS2 6LS; 01702 220400

Swansea College, Tyoch Road, Tyoch, **Swansea** SA4 9EB; 01792 206871

West Kent College, Brook Street, **Tonbridge**, Kent TN9 2PW; 01732 358101

Richmond upon Thames College, Egerton Road, **Twickenham** TW2 7SJ; 0181 607 8101

Hertford Regional College, Ware Centre, Scotts Road, **Ware**, Herts SG12 9JF; 01920 465441

Brooklands College, Heath Road, **Weybridge**, Surrey KT13 8TT; 01932 853300

Distance learning courses in PR and marketing

Frank Jefkins School of Communication, 36 Norfold Avenue, Sanderstead, Surrey CR7 8ND; 0181 657 3172

Guided Studies, 46 Mitchell Street, Birtley, County Durham DH3 1ER; 0191 410 7250

Martran College, 3 Nottingham Court, Covent Garden, London WC2H 9AY; 0171 379 1032

The Public Relations Education Trust, Public Relations Consultants Association, Willow House, Willow Place, London SW1P 1JH; 0171 233 6026

Public relations seminars and short courses

British Association of Industrial Editors; 01732 459331
CIM Marketing Training Seminars; 01628 524922/2229
Doug Goodman PR; 01879 771105
Henshall Centre; 0161 440 8466
Industrial Society (Communication Skills Department); 0171 839 4300
London School of Public Relations; 0171 584 4070
Public Relations Consultants Association; 0171 233 6026
Trident Training Services; 0181 874 3610

Higher and further education

Pre-entry courses

Bell College of Technology, Almanda Street, Hamilton, Lanarkshire ML3 0JB; 01639 283100

Cornwall College, Centre for Arts, Media and Social Sciences, Pool, Redruth, Cornwall TR15 3RD, 01209 712911

Darlington College of Technology, Cleveland Avenue, Darlington, Co Durham DL3 7BB; 01325 503050

Gloucestershire College of Arts and Technology, Brunswick Campus, Brunswick Road, Gloucester GL1 1HU; 01452 426549

Gwent Tertiary College, Pontypool and Usk Campus, Blaendare Road, Pontypool, Gwent NP4 5YE; 01495 755141

Harlow College, College Square, The Hyde, Harlow, Essex CM20 1LT; 01279 441288

Highbury College, Dovercourt Road, Cosham, Portsmouth PO6 2SA; 01705 283287

Lambeth College (for ethnic minorities only), Vauxhall Centre, Belmore Street, Wandsworth Road, London SW8 2JY; 0171 501 5424

Sheffield College, Stradbroke Centre, Spinkhill Drive, Sheffield, South Yorkshire S13 8FD; 01142 602700

Strathclyde University, 26 Richmond Street, Glasgow G4 0BA; 0141 553 4166

Institutes offering further education qualifications

HND, BA or postgraduate diplomas

Note: C = Communication Studies, J = Journalism, M = Media, PR = Public Relations

Anglia Polytechnic University *C*
Senior Admissions Officer, East Road, Cambridge CB1 1PT; 01223 363271; Angliaaccess@v-eanglia.ac.uk

Barnsley College of Higher and Further Education *J*
Administrative Officer, Client Services Team, Church Street, Barnsley S70 2AX; 01226 730191

University of Birmingham *M*
Director of Admissions, Edgbaston, Birmingham B15 2TT; 0121 414 3697; prospectus@birmingham.ac.uk

University of Central England in Birmingham *M J*
Perry Barr, Birmingham B42 2SU; 0121 331 5719

Blackpool and Fylde College *M*
The College Information Officer, Ashfield Road, Bispham, Blackpool FY2
0HB; 01253 352352

Bournemouth University *C J*
The Registrar, Talbot Campus, Fern Barrow, Poole BH12 5BB; 01202
524111; postmaster@bournemouth.ac.uk

University of Bradford *C*
Schools Liaison Officer, Richmond Road, Bradford, West Yorkshire BD7
1DP; 01274 383081;
ug-admissions@bradford.ac.uk

University of Brighton *M*
Admissions, Academic Registry, Mithras House, Lewes Road, Brighton
BN2 4AT 01273 600900 admissions@bton.ac.uk

Calderdale College *J*
The Percival Whitley Centre, Francis Street, Halifax HX1 3UZ; 01422
358221

Canterbury Christ Church College of Higher Education *M*
Admissions Officer, Canterbury, Kent CT1 1QU; 01227 767700

University of Central Lancashire *J M*
Centre for Journalism, Preston, Lancashire PR1 2HE; 01772 201201;
Department of Journalism: 01772 893730; m.s.hutchinson@uclan.ac.uk

Cheltenham and Gloucester College of Higher Education *C M*
Admissions Administrator, PO Box 220, The Park, Cheltenham,
Gloucestershire GL50 2QF; 01242 532824/6; admissions@chelt.ac.uk

Chichester Institute of Higher Education *M*
Academic Registrar, Bognor Regis Campus, The Dome, Upper Bognor
Road, Bognor Regis, West Sussex PO21 1HR; 01243 816000

City of Liverpool Community College *M*
Information Officer, Myrtle Street, Liverpool L7 7DN; 0151 252 4000

City University *M*
Graduate Centre for Journalism, Northampton Square, London EC1V
0HB; 0171 477 8028; r.s.broom@city.ac.uk

Colchester Institute *C*
Assistant Registrar, Sheepen Road, Colchester, Essex CO3 3LL; 01206
718000

College of St Mark and St John *PR M*
Admissions Officer, Derriford, Plymouth PL6 0DL1, 01752 636827

Coventry University *C*
Director of Corporate Affairs, Priory Street, Coventry CV1 5FB; 01203
838774

Cumbria College of Art and Design *M*
The Registrar, Brampton Road, Carlisle, Cumbria CA3 9AY; 01228 25333

De Montfort University *M*
Assistant Registrar (Admissions), The Gateway, Leicester LE1 9BH; 0116
2551551

University of East London *M*
Head of Admission and Student Finance, Longbridge Road, Dagenham,
Essex RM8 2AS; 0181 590 7000; cecilia@uel.ac.uk

Falmouth College of Arts *J M*
Admissions Office, Woodlane, Falmouth, Cornwall TR11 4RA; 01326
211077

University of Glamorgan *M*
Administrative Assistant, Pontypridd, Mid Glamorgan CF37 1DL; 01443
482225; admissions@glamorgan.ac.uk

Glasgow Caledonian University *J*
Scottish Centre for Journalism Studies, Cowcaddens Road, Glasgow G4
0BA; 0141 331 3000

Gloucestershire College of Arts and Technology *M*
The Registry, Brunswick Road, Gloucester GL1 1HU; 01425 426549

Goldsmiths College, University of London *J M*
Media and Communications Department, New Cross, London SE14
6NN; 0171 9197171

University of Huddersfield *C*
Schools and Colleges Liaison Officer, Queensgate, Huddersfield, West
Yorkshire HD1 3DH; 01484 422288; prospectus@hud.ac.uk

James Watt College of Further Education *J*
Student Advisor, Finnart Street, Greenock PA16 8HF; 01475 724433;
100065.3032@compuserve.com

King Alfred's College *M*
Senior Assistant Registrar (Admissions), Winchester, Hampshire SO22
4NR; 01962 841515

University of Leeds *J C*
Trinity and All Saints College, Leeds LS18 5HD; 0113 233 2332/01532 584341

Leeds Metropolitan *M PR*
Course Enquiries Office, Calverley Street, Leeds LS1 3HE; 0113 283 3113; course-enquiries@lmu.ac.uk

University of Lincolnshire and Humberside *C M*
Senior Admissions Manager, Central Admissions Unit, Milner Hall, Cottingham Road, Hull HU6 7RT; 01482 440550 ext 3504; tjohnson@humber.ac.uk

University of Liverpool *C*
Faculty Admissions Sub-Deans, Liverpool L69 3BX; 0151 794 2000

Liverpool John Moores *J C M*
School of Media, Critical and Creative Arts, Dean Walters Building, St James Road, Liverpool L1 7BR; 0151 231 5035; recruitment@livjm.ac.uk

London College of Printing and Distributive Trades *J*
Elephant and Castle, London SE1 6SP; 0171 362 5000

London Institute *M*
Communications and Marketing Department, 65 Davies Street, London W1 2DA; 0171 514 6000

Luton University *M*
Senior Admissions Office, Park Square, Luton, Bedfordshire LU1 3JU; 01582 489286

Manchester Metropolitan University *M*
The Applications Section, Academic Division, All Saints, Manchester M15 6BH; 0161 247 1035/6/7/8

Middlesex University *J*
Admissions Enquiries, White Hart Lane, London N17 8HR; 0181 362 5000; admissions@mdx.ac.uk

Napier University *J*
Information Office, 219 Colinton Road, Edinburgh EH14 1DJ; 0131 455 4330; j.sutherland@napier.ac.uk

North East Wales Institute of Higher Education *M*
Admission Office, Plas Coch, Mold Road, Wrexham, Clwyd LL11 2AW; 01978 290666

Northern Media School *M C*
Sheffield Hallam University, Pond Street, Sheffield S1 1WB; 01742 720911

Nottingham Trent University *J*
The Registry, Burton Street, Nottingham NG1 4BU, 0115 941 0410

University of Paisley *M*
Assistant Registrar (Admissions), High Street, Paisley PA1 2BE; 0141 848
3859; fras-apo@paisley.ac.uk

Plymouth College and Art and Design *M*
Information and Admissions Officer, Tavistock Place, Plymouth PL4 8AT;
01752 203444

Queen Margaret College *C*
Admissions Officer, Clerwood Terrace, Edinburgh EH12 8TS; 0131 317
3240; rgbutc@main.qmced.ac.uk

Roehampton Institute *M*
Admissions Officer, Senate House, Roehampton Lane, London SW15
5PU; 0181 392 3000

University of Salford *M*
Salford M5 4WT; 0161 745 5000;
admissions@univ-management.salford.ac.uk

University of Sheffield *J*
Department of Journalism Studies, University of Sheffield, 171
Northumberland Road, Sheffield S10 2JZ; 0114 282 6730;
ug.admissions@sheffield.ac.uk

Southampton Institute *J M*
Deputy Registrar, East Park Terrace, Southampton, Hampshire SO14 0YN;
01703 319348

South Bank University *M*
Central Admissions Office, 103 Borough Road, London SE1 0AA; 0171
815 8158; enrol@sbu.ac.uk

Staffordshire University *M*
Assistant Registrar (Admissions), College Road, Stoke-on-Trent ST4 2DE;
01782 294000; admissions@staffs.ac.uk

Suffolk College *M*
Assistant Registrar (Admissions), Rope Walk, Ipswich IP4 1LT; 01473
255885

University of Sunderland *M*
Student Recruitment, Unit 4C, Technology Park, Chester Road,
Sunderland SR2 7PS; 0191 515 3000; student-helpline@sunderland.ac.uk

The Surrey Institute of Art and Design *J M*
The Registry, Falkner Road, Farnham, Surrey GU9 7DS; 01252 732286
cbarter@surrat.ac.uk

University of Sussex *M*
Admissions Officer, Falmer, Brighton BN1 9RH; 01273 678416; ug.admissions@sussex.ac.uk

University of Teesside *J*
Admissions and Records Office, Borough Road, Middlesbrough, Cleveland TS1 2BA; 01642 218121; h.cummins@tees.ac.uk

University of Ulster *C*
The Admissions Officer, Cromore Road, Coleraine, Co Londonderry BT52 1SA; 01265 44141; jrc.mcafee@ulst.ac.uk

University College Warrington *M*
Academic Registrar, Padgate Campus, Crab Lane, Warrington WA2 0DB; 01925 494494; h.e@warr.ac.uk

University of Wales, Bangor *C*
Senior Admissions Registrar, Admissions Office, Bangor, Gwynedd LL57 2BG; 01248 382017/8/9; k102@bangor.ac.uk

University of Wales, Cardiff *J M*
Centre for Journalism Studies, Bute Building, King Edward VII Avenue, Catheys Park, Cardiff CF1 3NB; 01222 874786; prospectus@cf.ac.uk

University of West of England, Bristol *M*
Head of Admissions and Student Recruitment, Frenchay Campus, Coldharbour Lane, Bristol BS16 1QY; 0117 965 6261

University of Wolverhampton *M*
Admissions Unit, Compton Road, Wolverhampton WV3 9DX; 01902 321000; admissions@wlv.ac.uk

Yale College *M*
Wrexham Further Education Centre, Grove Park Road, Wrexham, Clwyd LL12 7AA; 01978 311794

Other training

Communication Skills Europe Ltd, formerly the Training Department, run a whole series of workshops for the public. Communication Skills Europe Ltd can be contacted at Paramount House, 104-108 Oxford Street, London, W1N 9FA; 0171 580 6312.

Fashion Journalism, Design and Promotion at the **London College of Fashion**, 20 John Prince's Street, London W1M 0BJ; 0171 629 9401

13 Useful addresses

Associated Press, 12 Norwich Street, London EC4A 1EJ; 0171 353 1515

Association of Independent Radio Companies Limited, Radio House, 46 Westbourne Grove, London W2 5SH; 0171 727 2646

BBC Corporate Recruitment Services, PO Box 7000, London W5 2WY; 0181 849 0849

British Association of Communicators in Business Ltd, 3 Locks Yard, High Street, Sevenoaks, Kent TN13 1LT; 01732 459331

Bureau of Freelance Photographers, Focus House, 497 Green Lanes, London N13 4BP; 0181 882 3315

Business and Technology Education Council (BTEC), Edexcel Foundation, Stewart House, 32 Russell Square, London WC1B 5DN; 0171 393 4444

Campaign, 30 Lancaster Gate, London W2 3LP; 0181 943 5000

Career Development Loans, FREEPOST, Newcastle upon Tyne NE85 1BR; 0800 585505

Central Press Features, Unit 20, Spectrum House, 32–34 Gordon House Road, London NW5 1LP; 0171 284 1433

Chartered Institute of Journalists, 2 Dock Offices, Surrey Quays Road, London SE15 2XL; 0171 252 1187

Civil Service Recruitment and Assessment Services, Alencon Link, Basingstoke, Hampshire RG21 1JB; 01256 29222

Communication, Advertising and Marketing Education Foundation Ltd (CAM), Abford House, 15 Wilton Road, London SW1V 1NJ; 0171 828 7506

Communication Skills Europe Ltd, Paramount House, 104–108 Oxford Street, London W1N 9FA; 0171 580 6312

Community Radio Association, The Media Centre, 15 Paternoster Row, Sheffield S1 2BX; 01742 795219

Department for Education and Employment, Sanctuary Buildings, Great Smith Street, London SW1P 3BT; 0171 925 5880/5882

Direct Marketing Association (DMA), Haymarket House, 1 Oxendon Street, London SW1Y 4EE; 0171 321 2525

EMAP Training, 57 Priestgate, Peterborough PE1 1JW; 01733 892444

Extel Financial, 13 Epworth Street, London EC2A 4DL; 0171 251 3333

Government Information Service (GIS), Marketing, Recruitment and Training Division, Information Officer Management Unit, Cabinet Office (OPSS), Horse Guards Road, London SW1P 3AL; 0171 270 123

Haymarket Publishing Group Ltd, 30 Lancaster Gate, London W2 3LP; 0181 943 5000

Independent Newspapers plc, Independent House, 90 Middle Abbey Street, Dublin 1; 01873 13 33

Independent Radio News, 1 Euston Centre, London NW1 3JG; 0171 388 4558

Independent Radio and Television Commission, Marine House, Clanwilliam Place, Dublin 2; 01676 0966 – statutory body with responsibility for independent broadcasting in Ireland.

Independent Television Commission (ITC), 33 Foley Street, London W1P 7LB; 0171 255 3000

Independent Television Network Centre, 200 Gray's Inn Road, London WC1X 8HF; 0171 843 8077

Institute of Public Relations, The Old Trading House, 15 Northburgh Street, London EC1V 0PR; 0171 253 5151

IPC Magazines, Training and Development Department, King's Reach Tower, Stamford Street, London SE1 9LS; 0171 251 5000

Irish Press Newspapers Ltd, Parnell House, Parnell Square, Dublin 1; 01671 3333

Irish Writer's Union, 19 Parnell Square, Dublin 1, Republic of Ireland; 01872 1302

London Business College, Distance Learning Foundation, PO Box 2998, London NW8 6EF; 0171 586 0084

London Chamber of Commerce and Industry, Commercial Education Scheme, Marlowe House, Station Road, Sidcup, Kent DA15 7BJ; 0181 302 0261

Morgan-Grampian plc, The Training Manager, Calderwood Street, London SE18 6QH; 0181 855 7777

National Council for the Training of Broadcast Journalists (NCTBJ), c/o Field House, Kinoulton, Nottingham NG12 3EH; 01159 455119

National Council for the Training of Journalists (NCTJ), Latton Bush Centre, Southern Way, Harlow, Essex CM18 7BL; 01279 430009

National Council for Vocational Qualifications, 222 Euston Road, London NW1 2BZ; 0171 387 9898

National News Agency, 30 St John's Lane, London EC1M 4BJ; 0171 490 7700

National Union of Journalists (NUJ), Acorn House, 314–320 Gray's Inn Road, London WC1X 8DP; 0171 278 7916

National Union of Students, 461 Holloway Road, London N7 6LJ; 0171 272 8900

The Newspaper Society, Bloomsbury House, Bloomsbury Square, 74–77 Great Russell Street, London WC1B 3DA; 0171 636 7014

The Periodicals Training Council (PTC), Imperial House, 15–19 Kingsway, London WC2B 6UN; 0171 836 8798

Pitman Training Ltd, 154 Southampton Row, London WC1B 5AX; 0171 837 4522

Press Association, 85 Fleet Street, London EC4P 4BE; 0171 353 7440

Radio Authority, Holbrook House, 14 Great Queen Street, London WC2B 5DG; 0171 430 2724

Radio Telefis Eireann, Donnybrook, Dublin 4; 01643 111 – Irish National Broadcasting service operating radio and television.

Reed Business Publishing Group (Training), Quadrant House, The Quadrant, Sutton, Surrey SM2 5AS; 0181 652 8032

Reuters plc, 85 Fleet Street, London EC4Y 4DY; 0171 250 1122

Royal Society of Arts (RSA), 8 John Adam Street, London WC2N 6EY; 0171 930 5115

Scottish Education Department, Awards Branch, Gyleview House, 3 Redheughs Rigg, Edinburgh EH12 9AH; 0131 244 5823

Scottish Newspaper Publishers Association, 48 Palmerston Place, Edinburgh EH12 5DE; 0131 220 4353

Scottish Vocational Education Council (SCOTVEC), Hanover House, 24 Douglas Street, Glasgow G2 7NQ; 0141 248 7900

Skillset, 124 Horseferry Road, London SW1P 2TX; 0171 306 8585

Thomson Regional Newspapers, Editorial Training Centre, Thomson House, Groat Market, Newcastle upon Tyne NE1 1ED; 0191 201 6043

UK Press Gazette, EMAP Business Communications Ltd, Maclean Hunter House, Chalk Lane, Cockfosters Road, Barnet, Herts EN4 0BU; 0181 975 9759

United Press International, 2 Greenwich View Place, Mill Harbour, London E14 9NN; 0171 333 0999

Universal Pictorial Press and Agency Ltd, 29–31 Saffron Hill, London EC1N 8FH; 0171 421 6000 – major international press agency.

Universities and Colleges Admissions Services (UCAS), Fulton House, Jessop Avenue, Cheltenham, Gloucestershire GL50 3SH; 01242 222444; applicant enquiries 01242 227788

Westminster Press Training Centre, Hanover House, Marine Court, St Leonards-on-Sea, East Sussex TN38 0DX; 01424 435991

World Entertainment Network News, 10 Vale Royal, London N7 9AP; 0171 607 2757

Writers' Guild of Great Britain, 430 Edgware Road, London W2 1EH; 0171 723 8074 (published writers only)

14 Further reading

More courses can be found in:

Floodlight – for the London area, on sale in newsagents
GET (CRAC) – on loan from libraries
Magazine Training Directory (PTC) – lists courses for training in periodical journalism

Reference books

Benn's UK Media Directory (Benn) – 2 volumes, annual
Willing's Press Guide (British Media Publications) – annual reference book with all publishers and their publications listed. Foreign guide also available.
Writers' and Artists' Yearbook (A & C Black) – yearly updates of publishers' names, addresses and publications. Covers rates of pay, working arrangements and copy writing.
The Writer's Handbook (Macmillan) – yearly updates of publishers' names, addresses and publications. Covers rates of pay, working arrangements and copy writing.

Newspapers and magazines with media interest

Aerial – The BBC's in-house magazine. Carries stories from within the organisation and advertises job vacancies. Available to BBC staff and visitors to BBC buildings.
Broadcast – news on production companies and programme developments.

Campaign, PR Week, Marketing Weekly – all cover the advertising and
PR areas of work, featuring new campaigns, movers and shakers
in the industry and current developments.
The media section of the *Guardian* – published every Monday, it
includes jobs and courses for journalists, plus analysis of the
current media industry. Particularly interesting are the features
where celebrities talk about how they made their break into the
industry.
Radio Ireland – radio and broadcast magazine, published by Maxwell
Publicity Ltd, MP House, 49 Waisfort Park, Terenure, Dublin 6;
01492 4034
The Stage and Television Today – weekly

Other useful publications

A Career in Magazines, frequently updated (PPA)
The Faber Book of Reportage (ed. John Carey), 1987. This book
contains reports on world events from Thucydides' account of
plague in Athens (430 BC) to James Fenton's report of the fall of
President Marcos in the Philippines in 1986. A great book to
study the reporter's art.
The Complete Reporter, Julian Harriss, 1981 (Macmillan)
Writing for the Press, James Aitchison, 1988 (Hutchinson)
The Online Journalist (Internet and electronic resources) Randy
Reddick, 1997 (Harcourt Brace College)
Modern Newspaper Practice, FW Hodgson, 1993 (Focal Press)
Writing Feature Articles, Brendan Hennessy, 1993 (Focal Press)
Dog Eat Dog: Confessions of a Tabloid Journalist, Wensley Clarkson,
1990 (Fourth Estate)
Practical Photojournalism, Martin Keene, 1993 (Focal Press)
Magazine Journalism Today, Anthony Davis, 1992 (Butterworth-
Heinemann)
The Freelance Journalist, Christopher Dobson, 1992 (Butterworth-
Heinemann)

Index